ANNOTATIONS TO THE FAMILY LAW (SCOTLAND) ACT 2006 (asp 2)

ANNOTATIONS TO THE FAMILY LAW (SCOTLAND) ACT 2006 (asp 2)

Kenneth McK. Norrie, LL.B, Ph.D, F.R.S.E.

Professor of Law, University of Strathclyde

DUNDEE UNIVERSITY PRESS
2006

First published in Great Britain in 2006 by
Dundee University Press
University of Dundee
Dundee DD1 4HN

www.dundee.ac.uk/dup

ISBN 1–84586–007–1
EAN 978–1–84586–007–3

British Library Cataloguing-in-Publication Data
A catalogue record for this book is available on request from the British Library

Typeset by Waverley Typesetters
Printed and bound by CPI Group (UK) Ltd, Croydon, CR0 4YY

CONTENTS

TABLE OF CASES

Page

TABLE OF STATUTES

INTRODUCTION

An Act of the Scottish Parliament to amend the law in relation to marriage, divorce and the juridisdiction of the courts in certain consistorial actions, to amend the Matrimonial Homes (Family Protection) (Scotland) Act 1981; to amend the law relating to the domicile of persons who are under 16 years of age; to make further provision as respects responsibilities and rights in relation to children; to make provision conferring rights in relation to property, succession and claims in damages for persons living, or having lived, together as if husband and wife or civil partners; to amend Part 3 of the Civil Partnership Act 2004; to make further provision in relation to persons entitled to damages under the Damages (Scotland) Act 1976; to make provision in relation to certain rules of private international law relating to family law; to make incompetent actions for declarator of freedom and putting to silence; and for connected purposes.

The genesis of this Act can be traced to a number of reports of the Scottish Law Commission: the Report on *The Law of Domicile* (Scot Law Com No 107, 1987), the Report on *The Grounds of Divorce* (Scot Law Com No 116, 1989), the Report on *Family Law* (Scot Law Com No 135, 1992) and the Report on *Title to Sue for Non-Patrimonial Loss* (Scot Law Com No 187, 2002). These reports were followed by the Scottish Office's Consultation Paper *Improving Scottish Family Law* (1999), the Scottish Executive's *Parents and Children: The Scottish Executive's Proposals for Improving Scottish Family Law* (2000), and finally *Family Matters: Improving Family Law in Scotland* (2004). As this diversity of roots suggests, this is really a Miscellaneous Provisions Act. It amends, improves and updates Scottish family law but only occasionally subverts or revolutionises the existing position. Of the 42 substantive sections, 28 amend existing statutes and only 14 provide rules for which the present Act will be the primary authority. Eight sections amend the Matrimonial Homes (Family Protection) (Scotland) Act 1981; four amend the Divorce (Scotland) Act 1976; four amend the Family Law (Scotland) Act 1985; two amend the Marriage (Scotland) Act 1977; two amend the Children (Scotland) Act 1995; and there are in addition single sections that amend the Sheriff Courts (Scotland) Act 1907, the Domicile and Matrimonial Proceedings Act 1973, the Damages (Scotland) Act 1976, the Administration of Justice Act 1982, the Law Reform (Parent and Child) (Scotland) Act 1986, the Adults with Incapacity (Scotland) Act 2000, the Protection from Abuse (Scotland) Act 2001 and the Civil Partnership Act 2004. The last mentioned is also substantially amended in Schs 1 and 3, replicating the amendments of the marriage and divorce legislation and correcting most (but not all) of the errors and omissions that entirely avoidably crept into the 2004 Act. Schedule 2 contains further minor and consequential amendments to many of the statutes already mentioned, as well as to the Civil Evidence (Family Mediation) (Scotland) Act 1995. The provisions in the Act that contain their own rule include the (partial) abolition of marriage by cohabitation with habit and repute, the removal of collusion as a bar to divorce, a new rule on revocation of special destinations on divorce or dissolution, a number of jurisdictional and private international law rules and (far and away the most far-reaching) a new set of rights and responsibilities to attach to cohabiting couples (ie conjugal couples who have not formalised their relationship with the state through marriage or civil partnership). It was the cohabitation provisions that led to the most wide-ranging and contentious debate at Stage 2 (Justice 1 Committee, 23 November 2005) and at Stage 3 (15 December 2005) but an overwhelming majority of both the Justice 1 Committee and the Parliament as a whole accepted the Executive's approach, and the amendments tabled to remove these provisions were resoundingly defeated.

The Family Law (Scotland) Bill was presented to the Scottish Parliament on 27 February 2005. The Committee to which the Bill was allocated for detailed scrutiny was the Justice 1 Committee, whose Convenor throughout its passage was Pauline McNeill, MSP (and incidentally an LLB graduate of the University of Strathclyde). Reflecting the party-political make-up of the whole Parliament, the Committee consisted of seven members: three from the Labour benches, two nationalists, a Liberal Democrat and a Conservative (the last-named also an LLB graduate of the same university). Though family law is a surprisingly politicised area of domestic law, such disagreements as arose among committee members seldom followed party lines. Though only a minority of the committee had any legal background, the private discussions and public debates were conducted in an informed and responsible manner (and with none of the rowdiness and political point-scoring that characterised the Westminster Parliament's debates on the (English) Family Law Act 1996, which rendered that Act unworkable in practice).

Stage 1 of the Bill involved the Committee spending some weeks in May and June 2005 taking evidence from a variety of interested bodies and individuals and giving consideration to a large number of written submissions. The Bill as presented and as discussed at Stage 1 was rather more limited than the Bill as eventually passed and the opportunity was simply not there for many provisions, introduced at Stage 2 or even Stage 3, to be given any consideration by respondents. Many other issues which were not in the Bill were nevertheless brought to the Committee's attention at Stage 1. Some led to amendments (such as the new provision relating to Jewish divorces (now s 15), and the amendment to s 11(7) of the Children

(Scotland) Act 1995 (in s 24)); others, after vigorous debate, were considered either not appropriate for legislative regulation (such as the *Charter for Grandchildren*, which was the Executive's response to the call from grandparents' organisations to encourage grandparents to have more involvement in children's lives) or not necessary (such as the call for step-parents to be given the power to acquire without court action parental responsibilities and parental rights). One rather disturbing feature of Stage 1 was the extent to which the evidence from pressure groups took on a distinctly gendered approach. Women's groups focused on the need to provide women and children with more protection against domestic violence, and they opposed the weakening of occupancy rights. Men's groups, on the other hand, focused on a problem that in both Scotland and England was receiving more and more media attention: the apparent inability of the legal system to ensure that contact orders in favour of non-resident parents (typically male), which are made with the welfare of the child being the paramount consideration, are actually enforced when the resident parent (typically female) refuses to abide by its terms.

More technically legal issues were brought to the Committee's attention by the written submissions and oral evidence of professional bodies such as the Law Society of Scotland, the Faculty of Advocates and the Faculty of Procurators and Solicitors in Dundee. The Bill as originally presented attempted to tackle the *Wallis* v *Wallis* (1993 SLT 1348) problem but did so clumsily and went further than was probably intended. The original draft of the new rules for determining the domicile of children was considered by legal professionals to be needlessly complex. The mess that the Westminster Parliament had made of the Scottish provisions in the Civil Partnership Act 2004 came in for stringent criticism and the Bill's attempts to clear up that mess were originally patchy. The various forms of powers of arrest, attaching to different types of interdicts, increased by the introduction in the Bill of "domestic interdicts", led many respondents to suggest that the whole area of interdicts and powers of arrest be substantially simplified. These, and other, matters were fully discussed in Committee and formed the basis of the Stage 1 Report which the Committee drew up in early summer 2005, broadly supporting the principles underpinning the Bill; many led to amendments at Stage 2 and Stage 3.

Immediately after the Summer Recess, the Stage 2 consideration began. Still in Committee, though with other (non-voting) MSPs often in attendance, this is the stage at which the actual provisions of the Bill (as opposed to its general direction) are given detailed scrutiny and amendments voted upon. Section by section, the changes to the existing law were examined and amendments to the Bill proposed, debated and then accepted or rejected. The consideration of the Bill sometimes concerned matters of detail (for example, the words used to define "child" in relation to civil partners), and sometimes matters of principle (as with a series of amendments, moved by MSPs not members of Justice 1, to remove the cohabitation provisions from the Bill entirely). One remarkable feature of the Family Law (Scotland) Bill was the large number of Executive amendments which were proposed at this stage. Partly this had always been intended: the Executive had openly accepted that in places the drafting was designed to generate a technical debate (as in how to solve the *Wallis* v *Wallis* problem), and it had accepted when the Bill was originally introduced that certain other amendments still required to be made (as in the corrections to the Civil Partnership Act 2004). But many amendments to the Bill were tabled by the Executive as a direct result of the recommendations in the Stage 1 Report: and these included matters of real import, such as the final abolition of the status of illegitimacy and the partial abolition of marriage by cohabitation with habit and repute. And many more amendments than had originally been thought necessary were made to the Civil Partnership Act 2004, to reflect the changes in the law contained in the Bill to its partner institution, marriage: some of these changes had not originally been recognised by the Executive as necessary. The opportunity at Stage 2 was also taken to introduce sections amending the Damages (Scotland) Act 1976, as recommended by the Scottish Law Commission in 2002, and to respond to wider changes such as the introduction at UK level of Pension Protection Funds. Amendment by amendment, section by section, the Bill was given as much time by the Justice 1 Committee as the parliamentary timetable permitted. The Stage 2 consideration of what was now a significantly larger Bill than had been introduced on 27 February 2005 came to an end on 30 November 2005.

The Stage 3 consideration of Bills takes place in the chamber of the Parliament as a whole. For the Family Law (Scotland) Bill, this occurred on 15 December 2005, when some final amendments were made and the Bill as a whole was approved. No parliamentary process is perfect and the time for discussion was often limited, but the Family Law (Scotland) Act 2006 improved almost out of recognition as it made its way through its various stages. The Act received Royal Assent on 20 January 2006 and it came into force on 4 May 2006.

1 MARRIAGE AND CIVIL PARTNERSHIP

SECTIONS 1–4 AND 42; SCH 1, PARAS 2 AND 10

Marriage is the state-sanctioned and state-registered relationship between couples of the opposite sex; it creates a status and is the identifier for a large number of public and private rights and responsibilities. Civil partnership is the state-sanctioned and state-registered relationship between couples of the same sex; it too creates a status and is the identifier of a large number of public and private rights and responsibilities. The two institutions have very similar consequences, and the rules for entering these legal relationships are virtually identical – other than that in addition to civil marriage, marriage but not civil partnership may be created by religious ceremony. The existing rules for the creation of marriage in Scotland are contained, mostly, in the Marriage (Scotland) Act 1977 and for civil partnership entirely in the Civil Partnership Act 2004. Until the Family Law (Scotland) Act 2006, however, most of the rules for determining whether a marriage or civil partnership was void for lack of consent were to be found in the common law rather than statute. The 2006 Act puts these rules onto a statutory basis. The Act has also taken the opportunity to update the law on forbidden degrees of relationship, to extend the jurisdiction of the sheriff court in consistorial matters and to abolish, if gradually and subject to a limited exception, the common law concept of marriage by cohabitation with habit and repute.

1 Marriage to parent of former spouse: removal of special requirements

In the Marriage (Scotland) Act 1977 (c. 15)–

(a) *in section 2 (marriage of related persons)–*
   (i) *in subsection (1), for "subsections (1A) and (1B)" there shall be substituted "subsection (1A)"; and*
   (ii) *subsection (1B) shall be repealed; and*
(b) *in Schedule 1 (relationship by affinity referred to in section 2(1B)), paragraph 2A shall be repealed.*

Schedule 1, para 2: Amendments to the Civil Partnership Act 2004

In section 86 (eligibility to register in Scotland as civil partners)–

(a) *in subsection (2), for "subsections (3) and (4)" there shall be substituted "subsection (3)"; and*

(b) for subsections (4) and (5) there shall be substituted
"(4) Paragraph 2 of Schedule 10 has effect subject to the modifications specified in subsection (5) in the case of a person (here the "relevant person") whose gender has become the acquired gender under the Gender Recognition Act 2004 (c. 7).
(5) The reference in that paragraph to–
(a) a former wife of the relevant person includes any former husband of the relevant person, and
(b) a former husband of the relevant person includes any former wife of the relevant person.".

Marriage

Before 1986 the forbidden degrees of marriage in Scotland basically followed the rules laid down in the Book of Leviticus. However, the Marriage (Forbidden Degrees of Relationship) Act 1986 amended the Marriage (Scotland) Act 1977 and removed many of the limitations on marriage that were not considered to be of any remaining social benefit. Of those that remained, the prohibitions on relationships of consanguinity and adoption are absolute, but the prohibitions on relationships of affinity (that is those created through another marriage) were qualified. In other words, two persons related to each other by affinity could indeed marry, but only if certain conditions were satisfied.

One of the qualified relationships of affinity was that contained in s 2(1B) of the 1977 Act, as inserted by the 1986 Act. This provided that a man could marry his ex-mother-in-law or his ex-daughter-in-law, and a woman could marry her ex-father-in-law or her ex-son-in-law, but only if they were both over the age of 21 and the marriage took place after the deaths of both the previous partners that created the relationship. For example, if Tom had previously been married to Margaret, he could marry Margaret's mother Ailsa, so long as both Margaret and her father Michael were dead. This rule always was anomalous. There was nothing to prohibit Tom and Ailsa living together, having sexual relations, or even having a child together during the lives of Margaret and Michael: the rule simply prohibited them from formalising their relationship as marriage (unless the conditions were satisfied). Section 1 of the Family Law (Scotland) Act 2006 removes the prohibition entirely. It did so timeously. The Bill (including this provision) had been presented to the Scottish Parliament seven months before the decision of the European Court of Human Rights in *B and L* v *United Kingdom* (ECtHR, 13 September 2005), where that court held the identical rule in English law (the Marriage (Forbidden Degrees of Relationship) Act 1986 being a UK statute) to be contrary to art 12 of the European Convention on Human Rights (the right to marry and found a family).

It is as well to note that this section does not remove all the affinitive relationships from the qualified forbidden degrees of marriage. Section 2(1A) of the 1977 Act remains as it was inserted in 1986 and that prohibits marriage between a person and his or her step-child unless (i) both parties are over the age of 21 and (ii) the younger party had not at any time before attaining the age of 18 lived in the same household as the elder party and been treated by the elder party as a child of his or her family.

Civil partnership

Virtually identical provisions relating to forbidden degrees were introduced for civil partners by the Civil Partnership Act 2004, s 86(2), (3) and (4); and Sch 10 (justified by the political need to subject civil partnership to the same limitations as apply to marriage, rather than by any pressing need referable to same-sex couples and their families). Schedule 1, para 2 to the Family Law (Scotland) Act 2006 repeals s 86(4) of, and Sch 3 repeals the appropriate parts of Sch 10 to, the 2004 Act, so that a person may enter into a civil partnership with their ex-partner's parent without satisfying any criteria additional to those set down for civil partnership in general. The step-relationship (which includes relationships created through civil partnership: 2004 Act, s 246) continues to impose a qualified bar on a civil partnership, subject to the same exception as for marriage: 2004 Act, s 86(3).

The rules for marriage and civil partnership interrelate, so that a person who used to be married may not enter into a civil partnership with the parent or child of their previous spouse (their step-parent or step-child) (Civil Partnership Act 2004, Sch 10); and a person who used to be in a civil partnership may not enter into a marriage with the parent or child of their previous civil partner (Marriage (Scotland) Act 1977, Sch 1, as amended by the Civil Partnership Act 2004 (Consequential Amendments) (Scotland) Order 2005, SSI 2005/623)). Again, these are qualified prohibitions which do not apply if the younger did not live in the same household as the elder and while being treated by the elder as a child of his or her family.

The substitution of the original subss (4) and (5) of s 86 with the new subsections here is designed to ensure that the definition of step-relationship is broad enough to include persons who have changed gender and are therefore no longer former "husband" or "wife". The prohibition is not avoided, in other words, by one of the parties having changed gender.

2 *Void marriages*

After section 20 of the Marriage (Scotland) Act 1977 (c. 15) there shall be inserted–

"*Void marriages*

20A Grounds upon which marriage void

(1) Where subsection (2) or (3) applies in relation to a marriage solemnised in Scotland, the marriage shall be void.

(2) This subsection applies if at the time of the marriage ceremony a party to the marriage who was capable of consenting to the marriage purported to give consent but did so by reason only of duress or error.

(3) This subsection applies if at the time of the marriage ceremony a party to the marriage was incapable of–

  (a) understanding the nature of marriage; and

  (b) consenting to the marriage

(4) If a party to a marriage purported to give consent to the marriage other than by reason only of duress or error, the marriage shall not be void by reason only of that party's having tacitly withheld consent to the marriage at the time when it was solemnised.

(5) In this section "error" means–

  (a) error as to the nature of the ceremony; or

  (b) a mistaken belief held by a person ("A") that the other party at the ceremony with whom A purported to enter into a marriage was the person whom A had agreed to marry."

Schedule 1, para 10: Amendments of the Civil Partnership Act 2004

In section 123 (nullity) (which shall become subsection (1) of that section)–

  (a) the word "or", which occurs immediately after paragraph (a), shall be repealed;

  (b) the word "validly" in paragraph (b) shall be repealed;

  (c) at the end of paragraph (b) there shall be inserted ", or (c) at the time of registration one of them who was capable of consenting to the formation of the civil partnership purported to give consent but did so by reason only of duress or error."; and

  (d) at the end, there shall be added–

    "(2) In this section "error" means–

     (a) error as to the nature of civil partnership, or

     (b) a mistaken belief held by a person ("A") that the other person with whom A purported to register a civil partnership was the person with whom A had agreed to register a civil partnership".

Marriage

Though s 5(4) of the Marriage (Scotland) Act 1977 lays down the legal impediments to marriage being celebrated in Scotland, so giving the district registrar power to prevent the marriage taking place, there have never been laid down in statute until now the grounds upon which a marriage that does take place can be considered void. One may assume that the impediments listed in s 5(4) render a marriage that went ahead void, but it has always been clear that these are not the only grounds. In particular, marriage is based upon consent and any challenge to consent is a challenge to the validity of the marriage itself. Section 2 of the Family Law (Scotland) Act 2006 puts into statutory form the common law rules relating to consent by introducing into the 1977 Act a new s 20A but, other than in one circumstance, it does not attempt to alter the common law rules. Though this new section is limited to marriages solemnised in Scotland, it is likely that a marriage abroad that would be void on the basis of lack of understanding or duress had it taken place here would not be recognised for reasons of public policy: see, for example, *Singh* v *Singh* 2005 SLT 749. Public policy is indeed given statutory effect by s 38(4), discussed below in Chapter 7.

A marriage is now statutorily declared to be void (that is to say null *ab initio* and of no effect) if one or other of the parties was either (i) capable of consenting to marriage but did so by reason only of duress or error or (ii) incapable of understanding the nature of marriage and of consenting thereto. Duress has been discussed in a number of cases involving very young women married off by their parents without their exercising any choice in the matter. It was held in the most recent, *Singh* v *Singh,* that the level of duress needed to be high: "a threat of immediate danger to life, limb or liberty, or some equally serious threat, is required before it can be said [in the words of Fraser *Husband and Wife* (2nd edn) at 444] that the party 'is compelled by force to marry or by some rational fear is terrified into compliance'." Error is limited by the new s 20A(5) to error as to the nature of the ceremony (for example, believing the ceremony to be a betrothal only, or to be a commitment ceremony without legal effect) or the identity of the other party. This is likely to have been the common law in any case (Clive, *Husband and Wife* (4th edn) at para 07.033).

The new s 20A(3) is worded oddly, and the second paragraph appears to be tautologous of the first because if a person is incapable of understanding the nature of marriage he or she is, by definition, incapable of consenting thereto. The primary issue is, therefore, capacity to understand the nature of marriage. The mental debility required is likely to be fairly serious, for the courts have traditionally regarded marriage as a simple, easy-to-understand, concept. Incapacity is to be determined at the time of the marriage ceremony. This might include temporary incapacity caused, for example, through drunkenness.

The change in the existing law is contained in the new s 20A(4), where it is provided that the tacit withholding of consent to the marriage at the time it was solemnised is not, in itself, a ground upon which the marriage is to be void. This is clearly designed to rid Scots law of the rule first established in *McLeod* v *Adams* 1920 1 SLT 229 where it was held that a widow who had married a rogue could have the marriage annulled on proof that the rogue never intended to lead a life with the widow as man and wife, but was only after her money. The extent to which this case underpins the "sham marriage" concept (a much more prevalent scenario) is not clear. This concept has allowed people to escape the marriages to which they purported to consent, on the basis that they were consenting merely to a paper act, a sham, a hollow charade but not consenting to the commencement of what the consenter intends to be a life-long loving and sharing relationship. Usually sham marriages are entered into for some ulterior motive (often connected to immigration) and the argument is usually that one or other of the parties has religious beliefs that the civil (or legal) aspect of marriage did not make "marriage" (in its true, god-created, sense) with the result that such religious beliefs can be used to defraud the legal system: see, for example, *Orlandi* v *Castelli* 1961 SC 113; *Mahmud* v *Mahmud* 1977 SLT (Notes) 17; *Akram* v *Akram* 1979 SLT (Notes) 87. The most recent example is *H* v *H* 2005 SLT 1025 where the Inner House overruled the Lord Ordinary who had held that consenting to a "marriage" as understood by the Marriage (Scotland) Act 1977 was all that was required rather than consent to "marriage" in the sense of a real, lasting, sharing and loving relationship. This decision cannot stand in light of the new s 20A(4). It is submitted that a person who purports to give consent to what the 1977 Act understands by marriage, but who for religious or fraudulent reasons believes in their own mind that they are not consenting to enter into a permanent relationship because such a relationship cannot be created by man but only by a god, is tacitly withholding consent to legal marriage. If this is so, then cases like *Orlandi, Akram* and *H* v *H* , as well as *McLeod* v *Adams,* are no longer good law. English law, incidentally, never took the approach in these cases: see *Vervaeke* v *Smith* [1983] 1 AC 145.

Civil partnership

Most of the above rules are applied to civil partnership by equivalent amendments to the Civil Partnership Act 2004. That Act provides that a person is not eligible to register a civil partnership in Scotland if incapable of understanding the nature of civil partnership or of validly consenting to its formation (2004 Act, s 86(1)(e)). However, as originally enacted there was no definition of "valid consent".

That omission has now been rectified. Consent is invalid if given by a person incapable of understanding the nature of civil partnership, or if given as a result of duress, or if given as a result of error. Error is limited to error as to the nature of civil partnership or mistake as to the identity of the other party (2004 Act, s 123(2), as inserted by para 10 of Sch 1 to the present Act). The effect of all of this is intended to be identical to the position of consent in relation to marriage, but the words are different and that intent may not have been given effect to, in at least two respects. First, "error", for marriage, means error "as to the nature of the ceremony"; while "error", in relation to civil partnership, means error "as to the nature of civil partnership". Now, the ceremony of marriage is different from the institution of marriage, just as the process of registering a civil partnership is different from the institution of civil partnership. For marriage, it is the nature of the ceremony that creates the institution which must be misunderstood before the marriage is void, while with civil partnership it is the nature of the institution itself that must be misunderstood. This could lead to a subtle, but real, difference between marriage and civil partnership. It was relatively common, before the creation of civil partnership, for same-sex couples to undergo commitment ceremonies, often in churches or town halls, which they knew would have no legal consequences. This remains all that is available to same-sex couples in many parts of the world today. Now, imagine a couple who, fully understanding the nature of civil partnership, wish to commit to each other personally but to avoid any legal consequence of that commitment. They travel to a foreign country and they undergo a ceremony of commitment. Unbeknown to them, however, that country has recently introduced a civil partnership law and the ceremony has unintended legal effects. They made no error as to the nature of civil partnership – they knew it well enough, indeed, to wish to avoid it – but they made an error as to the nature of the ceremony. On the unembellished words of the Act, this couple are enpartnered, even although had they been an opposite-sex couple who understood the nature of marriage but erred as to the nature of the ceremony there would be no marriage. The explanation for this difference in wording lies in the mean-spirited determination of those who instructed the drafters of the Civil Partnership Act 2004 to avoid at all costs words such as "ceremony", "celebration" and "celebrant" and to use the more sterile "registration" and "registrar". But given an overall intention to harmonise the rules, even when different words are used, is it possible to interpret the new s 123(2)(a) of the Civil Partnership Act 2004 to mean the same as the new s 20A(5)(a) of the Marriage (Scotland) Act 1977? It is clumsy, but desirable: "nature of civil partnership" in s 123(2)(a) needs to be interpreted, if it is to have exactly the same effect as s 20A(5)(a), as "nature of the process creating civil partnership". Otherwise a difference of no obvious benefit to anyone, and potentially disadvantageous for one type of couple over the other, will be part of the law.

The second, and perhaps less important, terminological difference between the marriage rule and the civil partnership rule is that a marriage is void if a party is incapable of understanding the nature of marriage "and" consenting to the marriage (1977 Act, s 20A(3), as inserted by the 2006 Act); while a civil partnership is void if either partner is incapable of understanding the nature of civil partnership "or" validly consenting to its formation (Civil Partnership Act 2004, s 86(1)(e)). However, as indicated above, incapacity to understand something brings with it incapacity to consent to that thing and so the "and" introduces no new rule of substance. "Or" is different and it is possible that a person is capable of understanding something but not capable of giving consent because age of consent is based on chronological age rather than mental maturity. A 15-year-old person may be capable of understanding the nature of civil partnership but incapable of consenting to its formation. But that incapacity is imposed by the specific age limit so "incapacity to consent" again adds nothing. There is, it is submitted, no practical difference between "and" and "or" in these provisions, and even if such a difference can be found, the courts are probably bound to interpret these single words to mean the same in this context.

Duress is unlikely to arise as an issue within civil partnership. The social circumstances under which civil partnerships are entered into may be somewhat different from those under which marriages are contracted (for example, family-arranged or forced civil partnerships are virtually inconceivable), but the principle of consent as a freely given and informed act must apply equally in appropriate circumstances and it is right, therefore, that the two sets of rules be the same even if needed more for one type of couple than the other.

A difference of rather more potential substance is the omission of a rule for civil partnership equivalent to the marriage rule relating to tacit withholding of consent (the new s 20A(4)). If this was the common law rule for marriage that took statute to remove it, there is no guarantee that the court will hold there is no such rule in respect of civil partnership. Yet while forced civil partnerships are unlikely, sham civil partnerships are (one may assume) every bit as likely as sham marriages. It is highly desirable that the courts do not recognise tacit mental reservation as a reason for nullifying civil partnership, but they must be careful to achieve that result for the right reason. It would be possible for the courts to distinguish marriage from civil partnership, because the former, with its long social and religious history, has an existence independent of the law, while civil partnership is created and governed only by the Civil Partnership Act 2004: the result would be that consent to marriage must involve consent to both the social/religious and the legal institution, while consent to civil partnership requires consent only to the legal institution. This argument is powerful, but demeaning. The courts should indeed resist holding that tacit withholding of consent to civil partnership is sufficient to nullify the validity of outwardly expressed consent, but they should do so on the basis that the common law marriage rule was anomalous and permitted frauds on the law and for that reason alone should not to be extended to civil partnership without direct statutory authority (which is, of course, absent).

3 Abolition of marriage by cohabitation with habit and repute

(1) The rule of law by which marriage may be constituted by cohabitation with habit and repute shall cease to have effect.

(2) Nothing in subsection (1) shall affect the application of the rule in relation to cohabitation with habit and repute where the cohabitation with habit and repute–

  (a) ended before the commencement of this section ("commencement");

  (b) began before, but ended after, commencement; or

  (c) began before, and continues after, commencement.

(3) Nothing in subsection (1) shall affect the application of the rule in relation to cohabitation with habit and repute where–

  (a) the cohabitation with habit and repute began after commencement; and

  (b) the conditions in subsection (4) are met.

(4) Those conditions are–

  (a) that the cohabitation with habit and repute was between two persons, one of whom, ("A"), is domiciled in Scotland;

  (b) that the person with whom A was cohabiting, ("B"), died domiciled in Scotland;

  (c) that, before the cohabitation with habit and repute began, A and B purported to enter into a marriage ("the purported marriage") outwith the United Kingdom;

  (d) that, in consequence of the purported marriage, A and B believed themselves to be married to each other and continued in that belief until B's death;

  (e) that the purported marriage was invalid under the law of the place where the purported marriage was entered into; and

  (f) that A became aware of the invalidity of the purported marriage only after B's death.

Of the three forms of irregular (and unregistered) methods of getting married recognised by the common law of Scotland since long before the Reformation, two were abolished by the Marriage (Scotland) Act 1939 but the third, marriage by cohabitation with habit and repute, was at that time retained as a method of entering into marriage other than by the formal processes now contained in the Marriage (Scotland) Act 1977. In essence it had latterly become a way of ensuring financial provision on death or separation to couples who had not in reality married (and who knew it). The law was willing to pretend that they had married in order to ensure access to benefits because it was often just and equitable that such access be granted. As such, it served some purpose in the absence of any other means by which unregistered couples could seek the law's protection. But the doctrine in the modern world was deeply flawed. Access to benefits was granted not when it was just but when the rules of the doctrine (designed for a bygone age) were satisfied. The requirement for habit and repute meant that those who benefited were those who were untruthful, or at least allowed a false impression to develop, about the nature of their relationship. The doctrine's history in the Canon law rendered it inconceivable that same-sex couples could access its benefits or that the courts would develop an equivalent form of irregular civil partnership. The fact that society had developed to such an extent that most unmarried couples live openly as such meant that the doctrine had less and less scope and provided a financial remedy for fewer and fewer people. And most importantly, the present Act finally gives financial rights and responsibilities to cohabiting couples (see ss 25–29 below), which removes virtually all remaining need for this ancient and anomalous doctrine.

This section therefore abolishes it, though gradually and in the event only partially. Any period of cohabitation that has occurred before the commencement of the Act can be used to found such marriage and as such it is theoretically possible for the courts to be dealing with marriage by cohabitation with habit and repute for upwards of the next 70 years. The doctrine is, however, unlikely to trouble the courts often since couples who do not marry by following the procedures in the Marriage (Scotland) Act 1977 will no longer need to rely on this doctrine to obtain some rights and responsibilities: they can apply directly to the courts for what they really want – financial provision on separation, and a share of the deceased's estate on death.

Section 3(3) and (4) retains the doctrine indefinitely in one limited circumstance: when the parties married abroad but did not expend sufficient effort to ensure that they followed the correct local formalities. As such, these subsections effectively overrule the decision of the Privy Council in *Berthiaume* v *Dastous* [1930] AC 79, and allow the court to hold that parties whose "real" marriage is invalid have become married by the doctrine of marriage by cohabitation with habit and repute. The scope of application of the doctrine is, however, remarkably limited and the conditions in subs (4) (which are in addition to the existing common law conditions) are to be carefully noted. The parties must have been married abroad, so a failure to follow Scottish requirements for a marriage in Scotland cannot be rectified by this provision. The parties must have mistakenly believed their marriage to be valid and the mistake must come to light only after the death of one of them: if they discover the mistake while both are still alive, their remedy is to get (properly) married and if one dies before this can be done the doctrine preserved by this provision is inapplicable. The deceased must have died domiciled in Scotland; the survivor must be domiciled in Scotland (presumably when the action for declarator is raised); the common law already requires that the cohabitation be in Scotland.

The common law continues to deny civil partners a similar means of rectifying foreign mistakes and the Act provides nothing equivalent for same-sex couples. And herein lies the major flaw in the partial retention of marriage by cohabitation with habit and repute. The problem that s 3(3) and (4) tackles is flawed foreign ceremonies and it allows Scots law to ignore these flaws in some circumstances. That result (which may be justified in itself) has been achieved through utilisation of a doctrine that was not designed for that purpose (there is no case in the law reports in which the doctrine has been used to save a marriage in these circumstances). The problem of flawed foreign ceremonies could have been resolved more easily by a simple provision that foreign flaws are to be ignored if discovered after death. The choice the Scottish Parliament made of the solution to the problem limits it to one type of couple only – opposite-sex couples – and excludes same-sex couples from its benefits. There are now dozens of countries that allow civil partnership, each with their own procedural requirements. A failure to follow a foreign formal requirement in a marriage is not fatal, but a failure to follow a foreign formal requirement in a civil partnership is fatal. Though it is not discriminatory to limit marriage as such to opposite-sex couples, it is arguable that to impose stricter conditions on same-sex couples who register their relationship abroad than on opposite-sex couples who register their relationship abroad is showing different levels of respect for the family life of each couple, as was the decision to resolve a limited problem through the unnecessary and clumsy mechanism of marriage by cohabitation with habit and repute.

4 Extension of jurisdiction of sheriff

In subsection (1) of section 5 of the Sheriff Courts (Scotland) Act 1907 (c. 51) (extension of jurisdiction), the words "(except declarators of marriage or nullity of marriage)" shall be repealed.

Consistorial actions were for many centuries limited to the Court of Session. Gradually, however, the jurisdiction of the sheriff court was extended, the most important extension being in 1983 when sheriffs were finally given the right to grant decrees of divorce. This section continues that trend by removing one of the remaining areas of exclusivity for the Court of Session. Section 5(1) of the Sheriff Courts (Scotland) Act 1907 provided sheriffs with concurrent jurisdiction with the Court of Session in actions of declarator, but excluded from this had been declarators of marriage or nullity of marriage. This section removes that exception and allows sheriffs to grant such declarators.

An important knock-on consequence of this, taken together with the time-limited and partial retention of marriage by cohabitation with habit and repute, is that sheriffs, when either s 3(2) or s 3(3) above applies, are for the first time empowered to grant declarators of marriage by this means.

Civil partnership was not constructed as a consistorial matter and actions for dissolution are expressly stated to be competent in the Court of Session or sheriff court (Civil Partnership Act 2004, s 117(1)). Declarators of nullity under chapter 6 of Part 3 of the 2004 Act (and presumably declarators of validity) may be made by "the court" which is defined in s 135 of the 2004 Act as the Court of Session or the sheriff. So no issue of exclusivity of jurisdiction arises with civil partnership and no amendment equivalent to that contained in the present section for marriage was necessary.

42 Action for declarator of freedom and putting to silence to cease to be competent

It shall not be competent to raise an action for declarator of freedom and putting to silence.

This old common law remedy was designed to allow a person, whom someone else alleged to be married, to establish his or her freedom to marry. The action was useful where an action for nullity was not available (for example, where there was no purported marriage to nullify) and was usually used to stop someone claiming that they were married to the pursuer. The Scottish Law Commission recommended the abolition of this action in its Report on *Family Law* (1992) (para 9.5) because it had been designed for a society in which marriages were not necessarily registered, and in any case today the normal remedy of interdict would achieve what was wanted. This section gives effect to its recommendation.

2 OCCUPANCY RIGHTS, INTERDICTS AND POWERS OF ARREST

SECTIONS 5–10 AND 32; SCH 1, PARAS 3, 5–8 AND 12

The Matrimonial Homes (Family Protection) (Scotland) Act 1981 was a statute of its time. In 1981 it was very common for the family home to be owned by one spouse only, typically the husband. This left the other spouse in a vulnerable position, for property law alone could not (nor is it designed to) redress the economic and social imbalance of power between the parties in the marriage. However, the 1981 Act aims to redress the balance to some extent, by giving a non-owning spouse (the "non-entitled spouse") the right to occupy the family home (called in the Act the "matrimonial home"). This was *not* a property right but it did and does constitute one of the most important effects of marriage, by conferring on both spouses the right to live in the family home, no matter which of them (in property law terms) actually owns the home. It is of course far less common today for a family home to be owned by only one, particularly within marriage and civil partnership, and typically family homes today are owned in common between spouses and civil partners. Property law itself, in that circumstance, recognises occupancy rights of both owners and special statutory provision is unnecessary. It follows that the dramatic effect of the 1981 Act is less noticeable now. Nevertheless it remains an important principle of law that married couples and civil partners (for whom virtually identical rights are given in ss 101–112 of the Civil Partnership Act 2004) both have occupancy rights in the home in which they lead their family lives (called, sensibly enough, the "family home" for civil partners).

Such occupancy rights are given real strength by further provisions in the 1981 and 2004 Acts for, as a general principle, occupancy rights are good against third parties and so cannot be defeated by the simple expediency of the entitled spouse or entitled partner selling or otherwise disposing of his or her own property. But the rights of third parties acting for value and in good faith require to be protected too and the Acts must therefore find an appropriate balance between two competing interests. The amendments in ss 5–9 and Sch 1, paras 3–6 of the present Act are designed to recalibrate this balance.

The other way in which families are protected under the 1981 and 2004 Acts is by providing special mechanisms to deal with domestic violence, an insidious and ancient problem in all societies. Again, the 1981 Act was a product of its time and was designed to encourage sheriffs to take the issue seriously by providing a form of interdict other than the common law interdict and by providing that with this new statutory interdict a power of arrest must be attached. No sheriff today needs encouragement to take the issue of domestic abuse seriously: the 1981 Act achieved its aim in this respect at least. And there is no longer a necessity for a special form of interdict to which a power of arrest may be attached, because the Protection from Abuse (Scotland) Act 2001 gives the court the authority to attach powers of arrest to all interdicts against abusive behaviour, whether they have been issued under the authority of a statute or otherwise. The Civil Partnership Act 2004 replicated the 1981 provisions here as elsewhere, other than the clumsy rules for unmarried – or unregistered – couples. For opposite-sex cohabitants the original 1981 Act allowed them to access the rules for "matrimonial" interdicts. The present Act amends in a number of important respects the rules in the 1981 Act for married couples and the 2004 Act for civil partners, and also provides similar but separate rules for unmarried and unregistered couples (for which see s 31, discussed in Chapter 5 below).

5 Occupancy rights: duration

In section 1 of the 1981 Act (right of spouse without title to occupy matrimonial home), after subsection (6) there shall be added–

"*(7) Subject to subsection (5), if–*

(a) *there has been no cohabitation between an entitled spouse and a non-entitled spouse during a continuous period of two years; and*

(b) *during that period the non-entitled spouse has not occupied the matrimonial home,*

the non-entitled spouse shall, on the expiry of that period, cease to have occupancy rights in the matrimonial home.

(8) *A non-entitled spouse who has ceased to have occupancy rights by virtue of subsection (7) may not apply to the court for an order under section 3(1).".*

Schedule 1, para 3: Amendments of the Civil Partnership Act 2004

In section 101 (right of civil partner without title to occupy family home)–

(a) *after subsection (6) there shall be inserted–*

"*(6A) Subject to subsection (5), if–*

(a) *there has been no cohabitation between an entitled partner and a non-entitled partner during a continuous period of two years, and*

> (b) *during that period the non-entitled partner has not occupied the family home,*
> the non-entitled partner shall, on the expiry of that period, cease to have occupancy rights in the family home.
> (6B) *A non-entitled partner who has ceased to have occupancy rights by virtue of subsection (6A) may not apply to the court for an order under section 103(1).".*

These provisions place a time limit on the rights of occupancy when the non-entitled spouse or partner is not actually exercising the rights. In other words, a non-entitled spouse or partner who is not in fact living in the matrimonial or family home loses the right to return and resume occupation in that home after a period of two years of non-cohabitation. It is to be noticed that two separate conditions need to be satisfied before occupancy rights are lost: (i) no cohabitation; and (ii) no occupation. "Cohabitation" is not defined for these purposes but it may be supposed that it means living together as husband and wife or as civil partners. A couple may continue to cohabit even when they are living away from the matrimonial or family home, for example because they are working or travelling abroad for a limited period with the intent of returning home: in that case the passing of two years does not affect the non-entitled spouse's or partner's occupancy rights so long as the couple were continuing to live together. Whether the non-entitled spouse or civil partner has "occupied" the matrimonial or family home while not living with his or her partner is a matter of fact, but the running of the two years may be interrupted even when occupation is not achieved by the non-entitled spouse or civil partner raising a court action to enforce the occupancy rights (see the amendments to the 1981 and 2004 Acts contained in s 8 below). It follows from the loss of occupancy rights under these provisions that the non-entitled spouse or partner cannot apply to the court for an order regulating occupancy rights under s 3(1) of the 1981 Act or s 103(1) of the 2004 Act.

6 Occupancy rights: dealings with third parties

> (1) Section 6 of the 1981 Act (continued exercise of occupancy rights after dealings) shall be amended in accordance with subsections (2) and (3).
> (2) After subsection (1), there shall be inserted–
> "(1A) The occupancy rights of a non-entitled spouse in relation to a matrimonial home shall not be exercisable in relation to the home where, following a dealing of the entitled spouse relating to the home–
> > (a) a person acquires the home, or an interest in it, in good faith and for value from a person other than

        the person who is or, as the case may be, was the
        entitled spouse; or
    (b) a person derives title to the home from a person
        who acquired title as mentioned in paragraph (a).".

(3) In subsection (3)–

    (a) in paragraph (e)–

        (i) for "sale", where it first occurs, there shall be
           substituted "transfer for value"; and

        (ii) for the words from "seller", where it first occurs, to
           the end of the paragraph there shall be substituted
           "transferor–

             (i) a written declaration signed by the transferor,
               or a person acting on behalf of the transferor
               under a power of attorney or as a guardian
               (within the meaning of the Adults with
               Incapacity (Scotland) Act 2000 (asp 4)), that
               the subjects of the transfer are not, or were
               not at the time of the dealing, a matrimonial
               home in relation to which a spouse of a
               transferor has or had occupancy rights; or

             (ii) a renunciation of occupancy rights or consent
               to the dealing which bears to have been
               properly made or given by the non-entitled
               spouse or a person acting on behalf of
               the non-entitled spouse under a power of
               attorney or as a guardian (within the meaning
               of the Adults with Incapacity (Scotland) Act
               2000 (asp 4))."; and

    (b) in paragraph (f), for "5" there shall be substituted "2".

Schedule 1, para 5: Amendments of the Civil Partnership Act 2004

In section 106 (continued exercise of occupancy rights after dealing)–

    (a) after subsection (1) there shall be inserted–

    "(1A) The occupancy rights of a non-entitled partner in
    relation to a family home shall not be exercisable in relation
    to the home where, following a dealing of the entitled
    spouse relating to the home–

        (a) a person acquires the home, or an interest in it, in
           good faith and for value from a person other than
           the person who is or, as the case may be, was the
           entitled partner; or

        (b) a person derives title to the home from a person
           who acquired title as mentioned in paragraph (a)."
        and

(b) in subsection (3)–

(i) in paragraph (e), for "sale", where it first occurs, there shall be substituted "transfer for value";

(ii) in paragraph (e), for the word from "seller", where it first occurs, to the end of the paragraph there shall be substituted "transferor–

(i) a written declaration signed by the transferor, or a person acting on behalf of the transferor under a power of attorney or as a guardian (within the meaning of the Adults with Incapacity (Scotland) Act 2000 (asp 4)), that the subjects of the transfer are not, or were not at the time of the dealing, a family home in relation to which a civil partner of the transferor has or had occupancy rights, or

(ii) a renunciation of occupancy rights or consent to the dealing which bears to have been properly made or given by the non-entitled partner or a person acting on behalf of the non-entitled partner under a power of attorney or as a guardian (within the meaning of the Adults with Incapacity (Scotland) Act 2000 (asp 4))."; and

(iii) in paragraph (f), for "5" there shall be substituted "2".

Section 6 of the 1981 Act and s 106 of the 2004 Act are designed to strike an appropriate balance between the rights of third parties on the one hand and the rights of the non-entitled spouse or partner on the other. The basic rule is that in a competition between a non-entitled spouse or partner and a *bona fide* purchaser for value, the former wins: so if the entitled spouse or partner sells the matrimonial or family home, the purchaser takes subject to the continuing right of the non-entitled spouse or partner, which defeats the purchaser's right to enter and occupy the home. *A fortiori*, if the third party purchaser is not in good faith (for example by knowing that the non-entitled spouse or partner had not renounced occupancy rights and that the entitled spouse or partner was attempting to defeat these rights). Of course, potential purchasers have well-known mechanisms to protect themselves from the risk of buying a house which they cannot occupy because of the non-registered occupancy rights of a non-entitled spouse or partner: purchasers now universally insist on the seller either signing an affidavit to the effect that there are no occupancy rights or providing a valid renunciation of these rights under s 1(5) of the 1981 Act and s 101(5) of the 2004 Act.

However, what remained unclear was the result of a competition between the non-entitled spouse or partner and the *bona fide* purchaser for value who purchases not directly from the entitled spouse or partner but from the third party who had previously acquired the property, whether in good faith or not, from the entitled spouse or partner. This fourth party would invariably require an affidavit from the third party but it is valueless since the third party (if in good faith) may not be in a position to know whether there is a non-entitled spouse or partner of a seller earlier in the chain. The purpose of the present provision is to put the matter beyond doubt and, at the same time, to shift the balance away from the non-entitled spouse or partner: the fourth (and fifth, and sixth) party now wins in a competition with the non-entitled spouse or partner, so long as he or she was acting in good faith and the transfer was for value. This shift in the balance may be justified as a reflection of the social shift since 1981 which has resulted in most matrimonial homes of spouses and family homes of civil partners being, in fact, jointly owned: occupancy rights traced to ownership are far stronger than occupancy rights conferred by the statutes.

Affidavits to the effect that there are no occupancy rights are replaced by written declarations and they may be granted by either the transferor of the subjects or a person acting on behalf of the transferor under a power of attorney or as a guardian appointed under the Adults with Incapacity (Scotland) Act 2000.

7 Occupancy rights: proposed dealings with third parties

In section 7 of the 1981 Act (court's power to dispense with spouse's consent to dealing and proposed dealing)–

> *(a) in subsection (1), at the beginning there shall be inserted "Subject to subsections (1A) to (1D) below,";*
> *(b) after that subsection there shall be inserted–*
>> *"(1A) Subsection (1B) applies if, in relation to a proposed sale–*
>>> *(a) negotiations with a third party have not begun; or*
>>> *(b) negotiations have begun but a price has not been agreed.*
>> *(1B) An order under subsection (1) dispensing with consent may be made only if–*
>>> *(a) the price agreed for the sale is no less than such amount as the court specifies in the order; and*
>>> *(b) the contract for the sale is concluded before the expiry of such period as may be so specified.*
>> *(1C) Subsection (1D) applies if the proposed dealing is the grant of a heritable security.*
>> *(1D) An order under subsection (1) dispensing with consent may be made only if–*

(a) the heritable security is granted for a loan of no more than such amount as the court specifies in the order; and

(b) the security is executed before the expiry of such period as may be so specified."; and

(c) after subsection (3) there shall be inserted–

"(3A) If the court refuses an application for an order under subsection (1), it may make an order requiring a non-entitled spouse who is or becomes the occupier of the matrimonial home–

(a) to make such payments to the owner of the home in respect of that spouse's occupation of it as may be specified in the order;

(b) to comply with such other conditions relating to that spouse's occupation of the matrimonial home as may be so specified.".

Schedule 1, para 6: Amendments of the Civil Partnership Act 2004

In section 107 (dispensing with civil partner's consent to dealing)–

(a) in subsection (1), at the beginning there shall be inserted "Subject to subsections (1A) and (1C),";

(b) after that subsection there shall be inserted–

"(1A) Subsection (1B) applies if, in relation to a proposed sale–

(a) negotiations with a third party have not begun, or

(b) negotiations have begun but a price has not been agreed.

(1B) An order under subsection (1) dispensing with consent may be made only if–

(a) the price agreed for the sale is no less than such amount as the court specifies in the order; and

(b) the contract for the sale is concluded before the expiry of such period as may be so specified.

(1C) Subsection (1D) applies if the proposed dealing is the grant of a heritable security.

(1D) An order under subsection (1) dispensing with consent may be made only if–

(a) the heritable security is granted for a loan of no more than such amount as the court specifies in the order; and

(b) the security is executed before the expiry of such period as may be so specified."; and

(c) after subsection (3) there shall be inserted–

"(3A) If the court refuses an application for an order under subsection (1), it may make an order requiring a non-

> *entitled partner who is or becomes the occupier of the family home–*
>
> > *(a) to make such payments to the owner of the home in respect of that partner's occupation of it as may be specified in the order;*
> >
> > *(b) to comply with such other conditions relating to that partner's occupation of the family home as may be so specified.".*

Section 7 of the 1981 Act and s 107 of the 2004 Act allow the court, on the application of an entitled spouse or civil partner or any other person having an interest, to dispense with the consent of the non-entitled spouse or partner to a dealing which has taken place or a proposed dealing on a number of grounds, both factual (the non-entitled spouse or partner is unable because of incapacity to consent) and judgmental (the consent is being withheld unreasonably). These sensible provisions allow an entitled spouse or partner to sell the matrimonial or family home to a purchaser who can take unencumbered by the occupancy rights of a non-entitled spouse or partner if the consent to the dealing (which would terminate the occupancy rights) cannot be obtained or is being withheld for no good reason. In *Fyfe* v *Fyfe* 1987 SLT (Sh Ct) 38, however, the sheriff held that it was competent to seek dispensation under s 7 of the 1981 Act only after price and other conditions had been discussed. In practice this removed much of the intended protection in s 7 (and now s 107) because a seller's inability to give the appropriate guarantees to a potential purchaser that the latter will take the property free of occupancy rights will virtually always prevent the parties moving on to discussion of other conditions. It is this limitation that the present provisions are designed to remove. Courts will now be able to grant dispensation of a spouse's or partner's consent to a dealing of the property during the negotiations, or even before. In other words, the entitled spouse now has a means of unencumbering his or her property before putting it on the market. This might be said to represent another shift of the balance away from non-entitled spouses and partners, but in fact it probably does no more than restore what was intended to be the position when the 1981 Act was originally enacted.

If dispensation is not granted by the court the non-entitled spouse or civil partner with occupancy rights could prevent the sale of the entitled partner's property, while enjoying the benefits of occupancy free. So another important amendment (recommended in the 1992 Report on *Family Law* (Scot Law Com No 135 at para 11.15)) has been added to s 7 of the 1981 Act and s 107 of the 2004 Act, allowing the court to order that the occupying spouse or civil partner pays for that occupation, or complies with any condition the court specifies. The court is not obliged to make such an order on refusal of dispensation and the balance of justice may require that no such order be made, for example if the non-entitled partner is bringing up the entitled partner's child who also lives in the home but has no means of earning an income.

8 Occupancy rights: effect of court action

After section 9 of the 1981 Act (provisions where both spouses have title) there shall be inserted–

"Reckoning of non-cohabitation periods in sections 1 and 6
9A Effect of court action under section 3, 4 or 5 on reckoning of periods in sections 1 and 6
   (1) Subsection (2) applies where an application is made under section 3(1), 4(1) or 5(1) of this Act.
   (2) In calculating the period of two years mentioned in section 1(7)(a) or 6(3)(f) of this Act, no account shall be taken of the period mentioned in subsection (3) below.
   (3) The period is the period beginning with the date on which the application is made and–
      (a) in the case of an application under section 3(1) or 4(1) of this Act, ending on the date on which–
         (i) an order under section 3(3) or, as the case may be, 4(2) of this Act is made; or
         (ii) the application is otherwise finally determined or abandoned;
      (b) in the case of an application under section 5(1) of this Act, ending on the date on which–
         (i) the order under section 3(3) or, as the case may be, 4(2) is varied or recalled; or
         (ii) the application is otherwise finally determined or abandoned.".

Schedule 1, para 7: Amendments of the Civil Partnership Act 2004

After section 111 (adjudication) there shall be inserted
"111A Effect of court action under section 103, 104 or 105 on reckoning of periods in sections 101 and 106
   (1) Subsection (2) applies where an application is made under section 103(1), 104(1) or 105(1).
   (2) In calculating the period of two years mentioned in section 101(6A)(a) or 106(3)(f), no account shall be taken of the period mentioned in subsection (3).
   (3) The period is the period beginning with the date on which the application is made and–

(a) in the case of an application under section 103(1) or 104(1), ending on the date on which–
   (i) an order under section 103(3) or, as the case may be, 104(2) is made, or
   (ii) the application is otherwise finally determined or abandoned,
(b) in the case of an application under section 105(1), ending on the date on which–
   (i) the order under section 103(3) or, as the case may be, 104(2) is varied or recalled, or
   (ii) the application is otherwise finally determined or abandoned.".

In *Stevenson* v *Roy* 2002 SLT 445 the Court of Session held that for the purposes of determining the time during which a non-entitled spouse was not in "occupation" of a matrimonial home, no account could be taken of the fact that, through court action, she had been seeking to exercise her occupancy rights. Occupancy was a matter of fact and once the non-entitled spouse had been out of the matrimonial home for the requisite period (at that time 5 years, now 2 years after s 5 of the present Act) she lost her occupancy rights. The effect of this was to give the entitled spouse or partner an incentive to prolong court actions and even defy court decrees. The present provisions amend the 1981 and 2004 Acts by providing that the running of the 2-year period in ss 1 and 6 of the 1981 Act and ss 101 and 106 of the 2004 Act are interrupted by the raising of an action under ss 3(1) (order regulating occupancy rights), 4(1) (exclusion orders) or 5(1) (variation or recall of either) of the 1981 Act, or the equivalent ss 103(1), 104(1) or 105(1) of the 2004 Act.

9 Amendment of definition of "matrimonial home"

In section 22 of the 1981 Act (interpretation) (which shall become subsection (1) of that section)–

(a) In the definition of "matrimonial home"–
   (i) after "means" there shall be inserted "subject to subsection (2),"; and
   (ii) for the words "one spouse for that" there shall be substituted "a person for one"; and
(b) at the end there shall be inserted–
  "(2) If–
   (a) the tenancy of a matrimonial home is transferred from one spouse to the other by agreement or under any enactment; and
   (b) following the transfer, the spouse to whom the tenancy has been transferred occupies the home but the other spouse does not,

the home shall, on such transfer, cease to be a matrimonial home.".

Schedule 1, para 12: Amendments of the Civil Partnership Act 2004

Section 135 (interpretation of Part 3) shall become subsection (1) of that section and–

  (a) in the definition of "family home"–
      (i) after "means" there shall be inserted ", subject to subsection (2),"; and
      (ii) for the words "one civil partner for that" there shall be substituted "a person for one"; and
  (b) at the end there shall be inserted–
  "(2) If–
      (a) the tenancy of a family home is transferred from one civil partner to the other by agreement or under any enactment; and
      (b) following the transfer the civil partner to whom the tenancy was transferred occupies the home but the other civil partner does not,
  the home shall, on such transfer, cease to be a family home.".

These provisions remove from the operation of the 1981 Act and Part 3 of the 2004 Act homes the tenancy of which has been transferred from the entitled spouse or partner to the non-entitled spouse or partner on their separation as a couple. In other words, if a couple separate and part of the separation arrangement is that the tenant transfers the tenancy to the other and subsequently moves out him- or herself, then the transferor, though now a non-entitled spouse or civil partner, may not exercise occupancy rights in relation to the house that used to be, but no longer is, the matrimonial or family home.

10 Matrimonial interdicts

  (1) Section 14 of the 1981 Act (matrimonial interdicts) shall be amended in accordance with subsections (2) and (3).
  (2) For paragraph (b) of subsection (2) there shall be substituted–
      "(b) subject to subsection (3), prohibits a spouse from entering or remaining in–
          (i) a matrimonial home;
          (ii) any other residence occupied by the applicant spouse;

(iii) any place of work of the applicant spouse;

(iv) any school attended by a child in the permanent or temporary care of the applicant spouse.".

(3) After subsection (2) there shall be added–

"(3) Subsection (4) applies if in relation to a matrimonial home the non-applicant spouse–

(a) is an entitled spouse; or

(b) has occupancy rights.

(4) Except where subsection (5) applies, the court may not grant a matrimonial interdict prohibiting the non-applicant spouse from entering or remaining in the matrimonial home.

(5) This subsection applies if–

(a) the interdict is ancillary to an exclusion order; or

(b) by virtue of section 1(3), the court refuses leave to exercise occupancy rights.

(6) In this section and in sections 15 to 17, "applicant spouse" means the spouse who has applied for the interdict; and "non-applicant spouse" shall be construed accordingly.".

Schedule 1, para 8: Amendments of the Civil Partnership Act 2004

In section 113 (civil partnerships: competency of interdict)–

(a) in subsection (2), for paragraph (b) there shall be substituted–

"(b) subject to subsection (3), prohibits a civil partner from entering or remaining in–

(i) a family home;

(ii) any other residence occupied by the applicant civil partner,

(iii) any place of work of the applicant civil partner,

(iv) any school attended by a child in the permanent or temporary care of the applicant civil partner"; and

(b) after that subsection, there shall be added–

"(3) Subsection (4) applies if in relation to a family home the non-applicant civil partner–

(a) is an entitled partner; or

(b) has occupancy rights.

(4) Except where subsection (5) applies, the court may not grant a relevant interdict prohibiting the non-applicant civil partner from entering or remaining in the family home.

(5) This subsection applies if–

(a) the interdict is ancillary to an exclusion order, or

> *(b)   by virtue of section 101(4), the court refuses leave to exercise occupancy rights.*
> *(6)   In this section and in sections 114 to 116, "applicant civil partner" means the civil partner who has applied for the interdict; and non-applicant civil partner" is to be construed accordingly.".*

As well as conferring occupancy rights on non-entitled spouses, the 1981 Act also created the concept of "matrimonial interdict" which can prohibit either an entitled spouse or a non-entitled spouse from conduct towards other members of his or her family, and can prohibit them from entering or remaining within a matrimonial home (1981 Act, s 14). Similar provisions for cohabitants ("domestic interdicts") are created by s 31 of the present Act, discussed below, and for civil partners ("relevant interdicts") by s 113 of the Civil Partnership Act 2004.

The amendments contained in the present provisions are important, but of fairly narrow scope. The major importance of the new substitutions is that they extend the places which a matrimonial or relevant interdict can prohibit a person from entering or remaining in. Prior to these provisions an interdict could extend only to the matrimonial or family home or a specified area in the vicinity of the matrimonial or family home. Yet a person who is a source of danger to a spouse or civil partner, or to a child living with the threatened spouse or civil partner, may as easily be a threatening presence at other places, such as any other residence, the place of work of the spouse or civil partner or the school of the child. Interdicts may now extend to cover these areas. However, the court may not grant a matrimonial or relevant interdict which prohibits the threatening spouse or partner from entering or remaining in the matrimonial or family home unless the interdict is ancillary to an exclusion order granted under s 4 of the 1981 Act or s 104 of the 2004 Act or the court is asked but refuses to grant leave to exercise occupancy rights, for otherwise this provision could be used to circumvent the more balanced provisions on occupancy.

32 Amendment of Protection from Abuse (Scotland) Act 2001: powers of arrest

> *(1)   Section 1 of the Protection from Abuse (Scotland) Act 2001 (asp 14) (attachment of power of arrest to interdict) shall be amended as follows.*
> *(2)   After subsection (1) there shall be inserted–*
> > *"(1A) In the case of an interdict which is–*
> > > *(a)   a matrimonial interdict (as defined by section 14(2) of the Matrimonial Homes (Family Protection) (Scotland) Act 1981 (c.59)) which is ancillary to–*

> (i) *an exclusion order within the meaning of section 4(1) of that Act; or*
>
> (ii) *an interim order under section 4(6) of that Act; or*
>
> (b) *a relevant interdict (as defined by section 113(2) of the Civil Partnership Act 2004 (c. 33)) which is ancillary to–*
>
>> (i) *an exclusion order within the meaning of section 104(1) of that Act; or*
>>
>> (ii) *an interim order under section 104(6) of that Act,*
>
> *the court must, on an application under subsection (1), attach a power of arrest to the interdict.".*
>
> (3) *In subsection (2), at the beginning there shall be inserted "In the case of any other interdict,".*

Before the Family Law (Scotland) Act 2006, there were different forms of interdict depending upon the different relationships between the parties – matrimonial interdicts for spouses (accessible in some situations by cohabiting couples), relevant interdicts for civil partners and common law interdicts for everyone else. Each had slightly different rules relating to powers of arrest that could be attached thereto. But this had been unnecessary since the coming into force of the Protection from Abuse (Scotland) Act 2001, which provided that powers of arrest could be attached to any interdict, and there were needlessly complex provisions ensuring that different powers of arrest were not attached under different provisions to what was essentially the same interdict. These complexities have all been swept away with the repeal in Sch 3 of the provisions dealing with powers of arrest in the Matrimonial Homes (Family Protection) (Scotland) Act 1981 in relation to matrimonial interdicts (ss 15–17), in the Civil Partnership Act 2004 in relation to relevant interdicts (ss 114–116), and in the 2001 Act itself preventing powers of arrest from being attached to two sorts of interdict against the same activity (2001 Act, s 6). As will be seen in the commentary to s 31 in Chapter 5, cohabitants will now also have their own form of interdict (domestic interdicts). However, powers of arrest are now to be located entirely within the terms of the Protection from Abuse (Scotland) Act 2001. If the interdict is sought by one spouse or civil partner against the other then, following the original rules in the 1981 and 2004 Acts but now contained in the new s 1(1A) of the 2001 Act, the court must grant a power of arrest; in any other case (including when a domestic interdict is sought by a cohabitant) the court must grant a power of arrest but only if two conditions are satisfied: (i) that the interdicted person has been given the opportunity to be heard by, or represented before, the court; and (ii) attaching the power of arrest is necessary to protect the applicant from a risk of abuse in breach of the interdict (s 1(2) of the 2001 Act).

3 DIVORCE AND DISSOLUTION

SECTIONS 11–20; SCH 1, PARAS 9 AND 11

The Family Law (Scotland) Act 2006 makes a number of amendments to the law of divorce (for married couples) and dissolution (for civil partners). These relate primarily to the grounds for divorce or dissolution, though there are also some important changes in relation to financial provision on divorce or dissolution and an odd addition to the law of divorce (but not dissolution) dealing with a problem created by some religious beliefs.

11 Divorce: reduction in separation periods

In subsection (2) of section 1 of the 1976 Act (irretrievable breakdown of marriage to be sole ground of divorce)–

> (a) in paragraph (d), for "two years" there shall be substituted "one year"; and
>
> (b) in paragraph (e), for "five" there shall be substituted "two".

Schedule 1, para 9: Amendments of the Civil Partnership Act 2004

In subsection (3) of section 117 (dissolution of civil partnership)–

> (a) in paragraph (c), for "two years" there shall be substituted "one year"; and
>
> (b) in paragraph (d), for "5" there shall be substituted "two".

The Divorce (Scotland) Act 1976 introduced into Scots law for the first time the concept of irretrievable breakdown of marriage as the sole ground for divorce and also, with rather more substance, the idea that a marriage could be proved to have broken down irretrievably simply through the passing of time during which the parties did not live together. The periods of non-cohabitation required to prove such breakdown were 2 years in the case of consensual divorce and 5 years if the defender did not consent to the divorce. In its 1992 Report on *Family Law* the Scottish Law Commission proposed reducing these periods to 1 year and 2 years respectively in order to allow marriages that were effectively dead to be terminated with less delay and (it was hoped) less stress than the existing waiting periods caused. The defender's ability to insist on a 5-year delay was used, more often than not, simply as a bargaining tool to be insisted upon or given up in the negotiations relating to the things that really matter – money and children – and there was no evidence that the delay saved marriages that would otherwise be brought to an end. The Scottish Executive accepted the force of these arguments, especially given the strong support from the legal profession for shortening the waiting periods, and the present Bill was drafted accordingly. However, the Parliament was not convinced that the case had been made out for quite such a radical reduction and so, at Stage 2 of the Bill's consideration, the periods were amended to 18 months in the case of consensual divorce and 3 years if the defender did not consent. The Executive's preferred position was restored at Stage 3 and enacted as such as an amendment to s 1(2) of the Divorce (Scotland) Act 1976.

The same reductions are made in relation to civil partnership by amending s 117(3) of the Civil Partnership Act 2004 where the facts amounting to irretrievable breakdown of civil partnership are listed – notice that they are identical to irretrievable breakdown of marriage other than the omission of the gender-specific and organ-specific (in Professor Thomson's pregnant phrase) concept of adultery.

It should be remembered (though it is not affected by the present Act) that since 2005, with the coming into force of the Gender Recognition Act 2004, irretrievable breakdown of marriage or civil partnership is no longer the sole ground for divorce or dissolution: in addition, the obtaining by one of the spouses or partners of a gender recognition certificate gives either spouse or either partner the right to an immediate termination of the marriage or civil partnership (allowing thereafter the person to whom the certificate refers the right to obtain a full gender recognition certificate which will effect a change in their lawful gender for most purposes, including marriage and civil partnership). The parties to the now-ended marriage will be able to re-partner with each other as civil partners, and the parties to the now-ended civil partnership will be able to re-partner as a married couple.

12 Irretrievable breakdown of marriage: desertion no longer to be ground

Paragraph (c) of section 1(2) of the 1976 Act (irretrievable break-down of marriage to be sole ground of divorce) shall be repealed.

In its 1992 Report on *Family Law* the Scottish Law Commission had recommended that desertion as a ground for divorce (or rather as a conclusive means of establishing irretrievable breakdown of marriage which was, when the report was produced, the sole ground of divorce) should also be abolished. The rationale for this recommendation was that if the periods of non-cohabitation as no-fault grounds for divorce were reduced to 1 year with consent and 2 years without consent, the need for a separate fault-based ground based on desertion followed by 2 years' non-cohabitation simply evaporated. Desertion was previously a means of obtaining a divorce without consent after 2 years, avoiding the need to build up 5 years of non-cohabitation. This provision gives effect to the recommendation of the Scottish Law Commission, as an inevitable consequence of the amendments contained in s 11 above.

The removal of this fault-based ground of divorce is a further step in the historical movement away from fault-based divorce that started in 1937 when the no-fault ground of incurable insanity became for the first time a justification for bringing a marriage to an end. The 1976 Act, though it expanded the concept of no-fault divorce, did not abolish fault-based divorce and is a conscious attempt to strike a balance between fault and no-fault grounds. Neither the Scottish Executive nor the Scottish Parliament in debating the present Act was minded to remove the fault grounds completely. So as well as non-cohabitation for the stated periods, and gender change, we retain the fault-based grounds of adultery and behaviour, which justify a divorce or dissolution as soon as the parties can get a date in court. It is the fault-based grounds rather than the non-cohabitation grounds that deserve to be described as "quickie divorces". The press and some Churches, so keen to retain fault as a concept, are, with a complete disregard for logic, the most vociferous opponents to what they perceive as "quickie divorces".

An equivalent amendment to the Civil Partnership Act 2004 is made by Sch 3 to the present Act, repealing s 117(3)(b) of the 2004 Act which provided desertion as a ground for dissolution of civil partnership. The ground never sat easily within the context of civil partnership in any case, because that institution never implied an *obligation* to live together. Marriage involved just such an obligation until 1984 when it was abolished, changing thereby desertion from a breach of obligation to the denial of an expectation. Overall, these provisions are sensible tidying of the law of both marriage and civil partnership.

13 Non-cohabitation without consent: removal of bar to divorce

Subsection (5) of section 1 of the 1976 Act (irretrievable breakdown of marriage to be sole ground of divorce) shall be repealed.

This section removes the provision in the 1976 Act that allowed the court in its own discretion to refuse to grant a divorce notwithstanding that irretrievable breakdown of marriage has been established by 5 years' non-cohabitation, if it was of the view that the granting of the divorce would cause grave financial hardship to the defender.

As a sort of safety net when non-consensual divorce based on 5 years' non-cohabitation was introduced in 1976, the Divorce

(Scotland) Act of that year gave the court the power to refuse to grant the divorce if the defender (that is to say the person not consenting to the divorce) would suffer, as a result of the divorce, grave financial hardship. This was explicitly stated to be "notwithstanding" that the marriage had broken down irretrievably. The caution of the law-makers in 1976 who permitted for the first time divorce on the basis simply of non-cohabitation was, perhaps, understandable but conceptually this provision was always problematical. For one thing, the court was permitted to protect the defender from grave financial hardship only in the absence of fault or consent: for this bar to divorce could be applied only to 5-year non-cohabitation divorces. For another thing, there was no guidance given to the court as to when it ought to exercise its discretion to refuse to grant divorce on the establishment of grave financial hardship. And finally, the bar lost what substance it had in 1985 with the enactment of the new rules on financial provision on divorce in the Family Law (Scotland) Act 1985: s 9(1)(e) thereof provides that one of the justifications for granting financial provision is to protect *either* party from grave financial hardship, whatever the ground upon which the divorce was pronounced. The removal of this bar by this section is overdue by 20 years, though in practice few will notice its demise.

The equivalent repeal in relation to civil partnership is contained in Sch 3 to the present Act, removing s 117(6) and (7) from the Civil Partnership Act 2004.

14 Collusion no longer to be bar to divorce

> (1) Any rule of law by which collusion between parties is a bar to their divorce shall cease to have effect.
>
> (2) Section 9 of the 1976 Act (abolition of the oath of calumny) shall be repealed.

Collusion is an agreement between divorcing parties to present a false case or to hold back a valid defence to divorce. It is a throwback to the pre-1976 days when divorce was based on fault alone and the "innocent" party lost their innocence (and was punished by being denied a divorce) if they agreed with the "guilty" party as to how the divorce was to proceed. Of course, nowadays, it is good family law practice for solicitors to encourage their clients to negotiate with each other, and indeed agree with each other so far as possible, including such matters as the ground to be used, and there was no remaining social benefit to be gained from retaining collusion as a defence which, in any case, was virtually unknown as a live issue in living memory.

This provision therefore tidies up the law by explicitly setting out that collusion between the parties does not bar their divorce on any ground. Consequentially, s 9 of the 1976 Act, which abolished the oath of calumny but provided that that abolition would not affect the law of collusion, is similarly repealed as redundant.

No equivalent provision is necessary for civil partnership because dissolution of that form of relationship never suffered the qualification of collusion and never knew (of course) the oath of calumny. That institution, and its dissolution, is entirely statutory and it would not have been open to the court to develop common law rules similar to any remaining common law rule affecting marriage.

For neither divorce nor dissolution will the court ignore the presentation of a false case, and abolition of collusion does not entitle the parties or either of them to found a claim on falsehood or facts that are inaccurate.

15 Postponement of decree of divorce where religious impediment to re-marry exists

After section 3 of the Divorce (Scotland) Act 1976 (c. 39) (action for divorce following on decree of separation) there shall be inserted–

"3A Postponement of decree of divorce where religious impediment to re-marry exists

(1) Notwithstanding that irretrievable breakdown of a marriage has been established in an action for divorce, the court may–

(a) on the application of a party ("the applicant"); and

(b) if satisfied–

    (i) that subsection (2) applies; and

    (ii) that it is just and reasonable to do so,

postpone the grant of decree in the action until it is satisfied that the other party has complied with subsection (3).

(2) This section applies where–

(a) the applicant is prevented from entering into a religious marriage by virtue of a requirement of the religion of that marriage; and

(b) the other party can act so as to remove, or enable or contribute to the removal of, the impediment which prevents that marriage.

(3) A party complies with this subsection by acting in the way described in subsection (2)(b).

(4) The court may, whether or not on the application of a party and notwithstanding that subsection (2) applies, recall a postponement under subsection (1).

(5) The court may, before recalling a postponement under subsection (1), order the other party to produce a certificate

from a relevant religious body confirming that the other party has acted in the way described in subsection (2)(b).

(6) For the purposes of subsection (5), a religious body is "relevant" if the applicant considers the body competent to provide the confirmation referred to in that subsection.

(7) In this section–

"religious marriage" means a marriage solemnised by a marriage celebrant of a prescribed religious body, and "religion of that marriage" shall be construed accordingly;

"prescribed" means prescribed by regulations made by the Scottish Ministers.

(8) Any reference in this section to a marriage celebrant of a prescribed religious body is a reference to–

(a) a minister, clergyman, pastor or priest of such a body;

(b) a person who has, on the nomination of such a body, been registered under section 9 of the Marriage (Scotland) Act 1977 (c. 15) as empowered to solemnise marriages; or

(c) any person who is recognised by such a body as entitled to solemnise marriages on its behalf.

(9) Regulations under subsection (7) shall be made by statutory instrument; and any such instrument shall be subject to annulment in pursuance of a resolution of the Scottish Parliament.".

This section is a substantial innovation into Scottish family law, and not one that appeared in the Bill as originally presented. The matter had, however, been consulted upon by the then Scottish Office in *Improving Family Law* (1999, paras 2.5.1 and 2.6), and the Scottish Executive's White Paper that followed (*Parents and Children* (2000) at para 8.5) indicated an intention to legislate in this matter. Shortly thereafter, the Divorce (Religious Marriages) Act 2002 dealt with the issue in England and Wales.

The issue is this. Many people of the Jewish faith regard "marriage" as both a religious institution and a legal institution, and they similarly regard divorce as a religious remedy and a legal remedy. Scots law partially reflects this by giving recognition to what the Marriage (Scotland) Act 1977 calls (at least in head notes) "religious marriages" as well as "civil marriages" (regular civil marriage is, indeed, a substantially younger sibling to religious marriage and did not come to Scotland until the Marriage (Scotland) Act 1939). But Scots law has never had any notion of a religious divorce: after the Reformation, exclusive jurisdiction in relation to divorce rested from 1563 in the Commissary Court and thereafter the Court of Session. The Commissary Court was, perhaps, a court of Canon law, but the process was always judicial. In the Jewish faith, the process of (religious) divorce is not judicial but is personal. This dissonance between law and faith means that a person in Scotland divorced by the courts may not regard him- or herself "divorced" in the eyes of his or her faith, and his or her co-religionists may not regard the person as free to re-marry within that faith – closing the door in practice to a further "religious marriage" even under the 1977 Act. This form of faith-based belief is not limited to the Jewish faith and is the reason, one understands, why the Duchess of Cornwall's second marriage could not be conducted according to the rites of the Episcopalian branch of Christianity. Freedom to re-marry within the Jewish faith is acquired not by court order but by "Get", which is a process of mutual consent to terminate marriage. If this mutual consent is withheld even in the face of a judicial divorce, some individuals may find themselves free to re-marry (civilly, or under the precepts of another religious body) in the eyes of the law but not free to re-marry in the eyes of their co-religionists (because a secular court cannot terminate the religious relationship also referred to as "marriage"). Frequently, the withholding of consent is used as a bargaining tool during the civil process to influence the financial settlement, and the future of children.

Once divorced by a court of law, both parties are free, in law, to re-marry. But the Executive took the decision, and the Parliament agreed, that the position of a divorced person who did not regard him- or herself as free in practical terms to re-marry within their own faith should and could be ameliorated. This provision gives the court the power (but does not oblige it) to postpone the granting of the (lawful) divorce until such time as the pursuer has taken such religious steps as are necessary to free the defender from the religious as well as the legal aspects of the marriage. It only works one way: when it is the pursuer who is seeking a legal divorce but refusing to agree to a religious divorce. If a defender is the one refusing the religious divorce then the provision actually strengthens his hand because if the defender does not want to agree to either type of divorce, a threat to withhold one type until he agrees to the other type is a threat to do what he actually wants. The provision promises more than it will deliver, for the person objecting to divorce is more likely to be the defender than the pursuer.

However, if the appropriate circumstances do arise, the court has this additional new power. If a pursuer seeks to use the judicial process of divorce but refuses to consent to the religious "divorce", then the defender may ask the court to postpone the granting of the divorce to the pursuer until the pursuer has done what he or she can to remove the perceived impediment to a subsequent "religious marriage". The court requested to do so must be persuaded that it would be "just and reasonable" to postpone the granting of the decree. It might be just and reasonable to do so if, for example, the refusal of the religious "divorce" is patently being used as a bargaining tool rather than as a reflection of genuine belief in the sanctity of marriage, or belief that the marriage might be saved. However, the fact that the refuser genuinely believes these things ought to prevent him or her seeking judicial divorce in the first place: a refusing pursuer will invariably, in other words, be in something amounting to or at least akin to bad faith. It is unclear where the onus lies (ie whether the applicant has to establish that it is just and reasonable to postpone the decree or whether the other party has to establish that his refusal of the religious divorce is just and reasonable) but it is submitted that, since the law regards freedom to re-marry as a just and reasonable and indeed inevitable consequence of divorce, any refusal to grant a Get by a pursuer who is nevertheless seeking a judicial divorce should be regarded, at least *prima facie*, as unjust and unreasonable (making the court's postponement of what the pursuer is asking for itself just and reasonable).

It is the concept of the pursuer being able to act to remove the impediment that limits this provision to those who profess the Jewish faith and who, as a result, would be regarded by others of that faith as not free to re-marry within that faith without the Get. While other faiths, such as the Episcopalian or the Roman Catholic forms of Christianity, do not recognise freedom to re-marry after a civil court has brought a marriage conducted according to the rites of these Churches to an end, that non-recognition is more absolute than with the Jewish faith in that it is not open to the parties to agree to terminate their religious "marriage". It remains to be seen, given the carefully neutral terms of the provision, whether it can be used by defenders attempting to force pursuers to "enable … the removal" of an impediment to remarriage such as undergoing a process that would lead to a religious annulment of the original marriage. And it is very much to be hoped that the provision has no effect over those of the Muslim faith where religious "divorce" is entirely gendered and the benefits of the section, therefore, would be limited to one gender over the other.

The court is also given the odd little power of recalling the postponement, whether or not either party has asked for it (subs (4)), but the statute gives no indication of when the court might wish to exercise this discretion. One assumes that the postponement will be recalled if the perceived impediment to remarriage is removed, but one would have expected recall in that situation to be required rather than merely permitted. The court may (but does not have to) order proof that the pursuer has acted sufficiently to remove the impediment (subs (5)). However, subs. (4) permits the court to recall the postponement on the application of either party or of neither and it remains to be seen the circumstances in which a court might consider it appropriate to do so. It may, for example, become apparent that the pursuer in a legal action of divorce has no intention of ever granting a religious "divorce" and the court may well feel that the defender's interests are best served by granting the legal divorce, resolving financial issues and then stepping back to allow religious processes to deal with a religious problem. It is to be hoped that no postponement is ever allowed to become, effectively, permanent.

This provision might be defended on the basis that it gives the defender a bargaining chip (an ability to agree not to seek a postponement) which balances the pursuer's bargaining chip (an ability to withhold consent to the religious "divorce"). But this redressing of the balance comes at a cost. This provision attempts to resolve a religious difficulty by the civil law and in doing so it conflates the notions of religious divorce and civil divorce. In a real sense it creates for the first time a legal notion of "religious divorce" (even although the provision is careful to talk simply in terms of removing an "impediment" to further religious marriage). But the provision is an acceptance that the legal process can and should be manipulated to allow individuals to by-pass immoveable religious doctrine. Though presented as a provision to show understanding of religious sensitivities it must surely undermine that very religious doctrine, for by providing a legal salve to a religious conscience it accepts that the law trumps religion. If people believe that, there should have been no need for this provision in the first place.

A defence of this provision, together with useful background information on Jewish divorce, may be found in D Levine, "Getting a Get in Scotland" 2006 JLSS 2/26, to which reference should be made by those advising Jewish clients undergoing divorce.

16 Financial provision: valuation of matrimonial property

In section 10 of the Family Law (Scotland) Act 1985 (c. 37) (which provides for the sharing of the value of matrimonial property and fixes the date of its valuation)–

    (a) in subsection (2), at the beginning there shall be inserted "Subject to subsection (3A) below,"; and

    (b) after subsection (3), there shall be inserted–

        "(3A) In its application to property transferred by virtue of an order under section 8(1)(aa) of this Act this section shall have effect as if–

        (a) in subsection (2) above, for "relevant date" there were substituted "appropriate valuation date";

        (b) after that subsection there were inserted–

            "(2A) Subject to subsection (2B), in this section the "appropriate valuation date" means–

            (a) where the parties to the marriage, or as the case may be, the partners agree on a date, that date;

> *(b) where there is no such agreement, the date of the making of the order under section 8(1)(aa).*
>
> *(2B) If the court considers that, because of the exceptional circumstances of the case, subsection (2A)(b) should not apply, the appropriate valuation date shall be such other date (being a date as near as may be to the date referred to in subsection (2A)(b)) as the court may determine.";* and
>
> *(c) subsection (3) did not apply.".*

In *Wallis* v *Wallis* 1993 SLT 1348 the court made a property transfer order requiring that the wife's half share in the jointly owned matrimonial home be transferred to her ex-husband. That had been a fairly common outcome on divorce, justified by a "fair sharing of matrimonial property" as required by s 9(1)(a) of the Family Law (Scotland) Act 1985, the property being valued at "the relevant date" (basically, the date of separation), and "fair" being presumed to be "equal" for the purposes. The problem was that the house in *Wallis* had increased in value substantially between the date of separation ("the relevant date") and the date of the decree of divorce, and so the effect of the order to transfer the wife's half share to the husband as valued at the relevant date was to give the husband *all* of the increase in value, even although the property was jointly owned. Had they simply separated and shared the proceeds of selling the house, both would have shared in the increase in value. The House of Lords held that this result was inevitable on the wording of the statute and it expressed only minor discomfort on behalf of the wife. But the result has been generally perceived as being unfair and as having led to a judicial reluctance to make property transfer orders that would otherwise be appropriate. The present section seeks to ameliorate that unfairness and to remove that reluctance by allowing the court to adopt a different date of valuation, though only in limited circumstances since the "relevant date" valuation remains in most cases appropriate and a useful mechanism for avoiding valuation disputes.

The new rule is as follows: in making a property transfer order the date of valuation of the property is not the "relevant date" but is either such date as the parties agree or, if there is no agreement, the date of the making of the order or (in exceptional circumstances) such other date as the court may determine as near as possible to the date of the making of the order. This departure from the "relevant date" rule is limited to valuation of property for the purposes of making a property transfer order within the context of a claim for financial provision justified by the "fair sharing" principle in s 9(1)(a) and as such may be seen in terms of giving the court the necessary flexibility to achieve that "fairness" that was palpably absent in *Wallis*. It is not, however, limited to jointly owned property, or to property transfer orders relating to the matrimonial or family home: it is to be remembered that other types of property may as readily fluctuate in value as heritable property. But "relevant date" valuation remains the only option for any of the other types of order available under s 8(1) of the 1985 Act justified by s 9(1)(a), that is to say orders for payment of capital sums, orders for sharing of pension lump sums or pension sharing orders.

The "appropriate valuation date", when applicable, may be agreed by the parties and it is only in the absence of such agreement that the court can set the date. But if the court does so there is a strong presumption that it will be the date of decree: only in exceptional circumstances (of which no examples are given by the Act) can another date be set and even then it needs to be as close to the date of decree as possible. "Exceptional circumstances" probably includes situations in which, for whatever reason, it is impossible to obtain a valuation as of the date of decree, but it is unlikely to include mere difficulty in obtaining such a valuation.

The rules in this section apply both to divorce for married couples and to dissolution for civil partners, for the Family Law (Scotland) Act 1985 has applied to both types of couple since the coming into force of the Civil Partnership Act 2004.

17 Financial provision on divorce and dissolution of civil partnership: Pension Protection Fund

(1) *The Family Law (Scotland) Act 1985 (c. 37) shall be amended in accordance with subsections (2) to (5).*

(2) *In section 8 (orders for financial provision), after subsection (4) there shall be inserted–*

"(4A) The court shall not make a pension sharing order, or an order under section 12A(2) or (3) of this Act, in relation to matrimonial property, or partnership property, consisting of compensation such as is mentioned in section 10(5A).".

(3) *In section 10 (sharing of value of property)–*

(a) *in each of subsections (4) and (4A), for "subsection (5)" there shall be substituted "subsections (5) and (5A)";*

(b) *in subsection (5), after "(4)(b)" there shall be inserted "or (4A)(b)";*

(c) *after subsection (5) there shall be inserted–*

"(5A) Where either person is entitled to compensation payable under Chapter 3 of Part 2 of the Pensions Act 2004 (c. 35) or any provision in force in Northern Ireland corresponding to that Chapter, the proportion of the compensation which is referable to the period to which subsection (4)(b) or (4A)(b) above refers shall be taken to form part of the matrimonial property or partnership property.";

(d) after subsection (8A) there shall be inserted–

"(8B) The Scottish Ministers may by regulations make provision for or in connection with the verification or apportionment, of compensation such as is mentioned in subsection (5A)."; and

(e) in subsection (9), after "(8)" there shall be inserted "or (8B)".

(4) In section 12A (orders for payment of capital sum: pensions lump sum)–

(a) after subsection (7) there shall be inserted–

"(7A) Where–

(a) the court makes an order under subsection (3); and

(b) after the making of the order the Board gives the trustees or managers of the scheme a notice under section 160 of the Pensions Act 2004 (c. 35) ("the 2004 Act"), or the Northern Ireland provision, in relation to the scheme,

the order shall, on the giving of such notice, be recalled.

(7B) Subsection (7C) applies where–

(a) the court makes an order under subsection (2) imposing requirements on the trustees or managers of an occupational pension scheme; and

(b) after the making of the order the Board gives the trustees or managers of the scheme a notice under section 160 of the 2004 Act, or the Northern Ireland provision, in relation to the scheme.

(7C) The order shall have effect from the time when the notice is given–

(a) as if–

(i) references to the trustees or managers of the scheme were references to the Board; and

(ii) references to any lump sum to which the person with benefits under a pension arrangement is or might become entitled under the scheme were references to the amount of any compensation payable under that Chapter of the 2004 Act, or the Northern Ireland provision, to which that person is or might become entitled in respect of the lump sum; and

(b) subject to such other modifications as may be prescribed by regulations by the Scottish Ministers.";

(b) in subsection (9), for "subsection" there shall be substituted "subsections (7C)(b) and"; and

(c) after subsection (10) there shall be added–

"(11) In subsections (7A) to (7C) "the Northern Ireland provision", in relation to a provision of the 2004 Act, means any provision in force in Northern Ireland corresponding to the provision of that Act.".

(5) In section 16 (agreements on financial provision), after subsection (2A) there shall be inserted–

"(2B) Subsection (2C) applies where–

(a) the parties to a marriage or the partners in a civil partnership have entered into an agreement as to financial provision to be made on divorce or on dissolution of the civil partnership; and

(b) the agreement includes provision in respect of a person's rights or interests or benefits under an occupational pension scheme.

(2C) The Board of the Pension Protection Fund's subsequently assuming responsibility for the occupational pension scheme in accordance with Chapter 3 of Part 2 of the Pensions Act 2004 (c. 35) or any provision in force in Northern Ireland corresponding to that Chapter shall not affect–

(a) the power of the court under subsection (1)(b) to make an order setting aside or varying the agreement or any term of it;

(b) on an appeal, the powers of the appeal court in relation to the order.".

The Pensions Act 2004 set up a Pension Protection Fund, run by a Pension Protection Board. The aim is to protect members of eligible private sector pension schemes from the risks of their employer becoming insolvent and thus unable to continue to pay their dues in terms of the scheme. Under the Act, if a pension scheme is unable to meets its commitments to its members, both its assets and its liabilities will be transferred to the Pension Protection Fund, and the Pension Protection Board will be able to pay compensation to the members. This compensation is not, however, itself a pension and so any statutory entitlement under the 2004 Act would not be available for pension sharing on divorce under the Family Law (Scotland) Act 1985. The purpose of the present section is to allow that compensation to be shared on the same basis. It amends s 10 of the 1985 Act (sharing of value of matrimonial property) by adding a new s 10(5A) which ensures that the proportion of the compensation due from the Pension Protection Fund that is referable to the period of the marriage or civil partnership will be treated as "matrimonial property" or "partnership property" for the purposes of fair sharing under s 9(1)(a). Pension lump sums (covered by s 12A of the 1985 Act) are also affected and if the pension fund assets are transferred to the Pension Protection Board, any orders under s 12A(3) to pay any part of the pension to the other party to the marriage or civil partnership are recalled, and any orders under s 12A(2) imposing requirements on the trustees or managers of the pension fund are altered so that these requirements are imposed on the Pension Protection Board instead of the trustees or managers. The fact that the Pension Protection Board has taken over responsibility for the pension scheme does not affect the power of the court to set aside or vary any agreement the parties have made which includes provision in respect of one or other's rights under an occupational pension scheme.

18 Financial provision: incidental orders

In subsection (2) of section 14 of the Family Law (Scotland) Act 1985 (c. 37) (incidental orders), after paragraph (j) there shall be inserted–

> *"(ja) in relation to a deed relating to moveable property, an order dispensing with the execution of the deed by the grantor and directing the sheriff clerk to execute the deed;".*

Sheriff clerks already have the power to execute deeds relating to heritable property if this is necessary to give effect to an order for financial provision (Sheriff Courts (Scotland) Act 1907, s 5A) and this new provision grants sheriff clerks that same power in relation to moveable property. So an order for the transfer of moveable property from one ex-spouse or ex-civil partner to the other may be effected even when the owner of the property refuses to comply. (The Court of Session has equivalent, inherent, powers.)

19 Special destinations: revocation on divorce or annulment

(1) Subsections (2) and (3) apply where–
  (a) heritable property is held in the name of–
    (i) a person ("A") and A's spouse ("B") and the survivor of them;
    (ii) A, B and another person and the survivor or survivors of them;
    (iii) A with a special destination on A's death, in favour of B;
  (b) A and B's marriage is terminated by divorce or annulment; and
  (c) after the divorce or annulment A dies.
(2) In relation to the succession to A's heritable property (or part of it) under the destination, B shall be deemed to have failed to survive A.

(3) If a person has in good faith and for value (whether by purchase or otherwise) acquired title to the heritable property, the title so acquired shall not be challengeable on the ground that, by virtue of subsection (2), the property falls to the estate of A.

(4) Subsection (2) shall not apply if the destination specifies that B is to take under the destination despite the termination of A and B's marriage by divorce or annulment.

Schedule 1, para 11: Amendments of the Civil Partnership Act 2004

After section 124 there shall be inserted–

Special destinations: revocation on dissolution or annulment

"124A Special destinations: revocation on dissolution or annulment

(1) Subsections (2) and (3) apply where–
   (a) heritable property is held in the name of–
      (i) a person ("A") and A's civil partner ("B") and the survivor of them;
      (ii) A, B and another person and the survivor or survivors of them;
      (iii) A with a special destination on A's death, in favour of B;
   (b) A and B's civil partnership is terminated by dissolution or annulment; and
   (c) after the dissolution or annulment A dies.

(2) In relation to the succession to A's heritable property (or part of it) under the destination, B shall be deemed to have failed to survive A.

(3) If a person has in good faith and for value (whether by purchase or otherwise) acquired title to the heritable property, the title so acquired shall not be challengeable on the ground that, by virtue of subsection (2), the property falls to the estate of A.

(4) Subsection (2) shall not apply if the destination specifies that B is to take under the destination despite the termination of A and B's civil partnership by dissolution or annulment.

It is very common today for couples who are married or in civil partnership to own their family home jointly, and usually title is taken with a survivorship clause: title inheres in "A and B and the survivor". Or if the family home is purchased in the name of A alone the title often contains a special destination in favour of B. In either case on the death of A, B takes the property irrespective of the destination of A's estate, for a survivorship clause effectively removes the family home from the estate to which the executor confirms. On divorce or dissolution, however, particularly where there is general agreement and no litigation over financial provision, the terms of the title deeds are sometimes forgotten. This is most likely when title is in the name of A alone with a special destination in favour of his or her spouse or civil partner, and it is amicably agreed on separation that both parties should retain their own property. The problem arises if the special destination is not, on divorce or dissolution, evacuated. It may be that A re-marries and some years later dies testate, leaving everything he owns to his widow. If the special destination had not been evacuated on the earlier divorce, his widow will be shocked to learn that it now removes the family home from the deceased's estate and transfers that home to the previous spouse or civil partner, from whom the deceased was divorced many years previously.

The present provisions deem the previous spouse or civil partner to have predeceased the deceased if the marriage or civil partnership is terminated by divorce or dissolution or annulment, with the result that the survivorship clause or special destination is not given effect to. This is subject to the qualification that the destination may itself provide that it survives divorce or dissolution or annulment. And third parties who have acquired the property which was subject to a survivorship clause or special destination are protected if they are in good faith and the acquisition was for value.

20 *Variations of agreements on aliment: power of court*

(1) Section 7 of the Family Law (Scotland) Act 1985 (c. 37) (agreements on aliment) shall be amended as follows.

(2) After subsection (2) there shall be inserted–

"(2ZA)   On an application under subsection (2) above, the court may–

> *(a) pending determination of the application make such interim order as it thinks fit;*
>
> *(b) make an order backdating a variation of the amount payable under the agreement to–*
>> *(i) the date of the application or such later date as the court thinks fit; or*
>> *(ii) on special cause shown, a date prior to the date of the application.*

(2ZB) Where the court makes an order under subsection (2ZA)(b) above, it may order any sums paid under the agreement to be repaid on such terms (including terms relating to repayment by instalments) as the court thinks fit.

(2ZC) Nothing in subsection (2ZA) shall empower the court to substitute a lump sum for a periodical payment.".

(3) In subsection (4), for "subsection (2) above" there shall be substituted "this section".

Section 7(2) of the Family Law (Scotland) Act 1985 allows for the making of an application to court to vary the amount of aliment that is being paid under the terms of an agreement. There was, however, no power for the court to make an interim order pending determination of a s 7(2) application, nor power to make an order backdating any variation that the court made in the order. As was pointed out by Sheriff Principal Maguire in *Woolley* v *Strachan* 1997 SLT (Sh Ct) 88, the court's powers in s 7 to vary an agreement on aliment were more constrained than its power in s 5 to vary an earlier court order relating to aliment. The effect of this was that it was in the interests of the payer who feared that a court order will make him or her pay more than was specified in the agreement to delay the determination of the application, and there was no sanction against the payer who hid from the payee an improvement in his or her circumstances. This section, by adding new subsections to s 7, removes these anomalies, but is careful to ensure that the nature of the payment (periodical allowance or lump sum), as opposed to the amount, cannot be varied under the new rules.

4 CHILDREN

SECTIONS 21–24

Notwithstanding the powerful political imperative of the Scottish Executive (and before it the Scottish Office), and the parliamentarians in the Scottish Parliament, to claim that all family law reform is about making life better for Scotland's children, the truth of the matter is that the present Act is not primarily about children at all, but about adults. One can understand that the law might structure the grounds for divorce in such a way that advantages or disadvantages children, that cohabitants' rights (or lack of them) will affect any children that there are, but given that marriage, civil partnership, divorce and cohabitation all exist and are phenomena requiring regulation independent of children, the reality of the reforms of these areas is that while children may validly be taken into account, the reforms are not primarily designed for them. The Family Law (Scotland) Act 2006 is *not* a new Children (Scotland) Act.

The Act does, however, contain a few provisions that are of direct relevance to children and these are found in ss 21–24.

Section 21 Abolition of status of illegitimacy

(1) *The Law Reform (Parent and Child) (Scotland) Act 1986 (c. 9) shall be amended in accordance with subsections (2) to (4).*

(2) *In section 1 (legal equality of children)–*

    (a) *for subsection (1) there shall be substituted–*

    "(1) No person whose status is governed by Scots law shall be illegitimate; and accordingly the fact that a person's parents are not or have not been married to each other shall be left out of account in–

        (a) *determining the person's legal status; or*

        (b) *establishing the legal relationship between the person and any other person.";*

    (b) *in subsection (4), in paragraph (a), for the words from "this", where it first occurs, to the end of that paragraph there shall be substituted "section 21 of the Family Law (Scotland) Act 2006 (asp 2)."; and*

    (c) *after that subsection there shall be added–*

        "(5) In subsection (4), "enactment" includes an Act of the Scottish Parliament.

        (6) *It shall no longer be competent to bring an action for declarator of legitimacy, legitimation or illegitimacy.".*

(3) The title of section 1 shall become "Abolition of status of illegitimacy".

(4) In subsection (1) of section 9 (savings and supplementary provisions)–

> *(a) in paragraph (c), at the end, there shall be inserted "(including, in particular, the competence of bringing an action of declarator of legitimacy, legitimation or illegitimacy in connection with such succession or devolution"; and*
>
> *(b) after that paragraph there shall be inserted–*
>
>> *"(ca) affect the functions of the Lord Lyon King of Arms so far as relating to the granting of arms;".*

For many centuries a person's civil status was affected by whether or not he or she was "legitimate" or "illegitimate". Most disadvantages and civil disabilities that flowed from "illegitimacy" were progressively removed by statute from the early 19th century and by 1986 it was possible for statute to provide that the fact that a person's parents are not or have not been married to one another was to be left out of account in establishing the legal relationship between the person and any other person: Law Reform (Parent and Child) (Scotland) Act 1986, s 1(1), as originally enacted. That Act did not, however, abolish the status of "illegitimacy" and expressly excluded from s 1(1) were the rules for determining the child's domicile and the rules governing the transmission on death of titles, coats of arms, honours and dignities (1986 Act, s 9(1)(a) and (c) respectively). More importantly than either, however, was the implicit qualification that a person's relationship with his or her father remained seriously affected depending upon whether the father was married to the mother or not, for a father who was not married to the mother of his child did not automatically acquire parental responsibilities and parental rights over the child. As well, statutes such as the Adoption (Scotland) Act 1978 continued to refer to "legitimate" children, and the "legitimation" of "illegitimate" children remained possible by a variety of means.

The present Act removes virtually all of the remaining effects of "illegitimacy": the new rules for determining a child's domicile in s 22 make no distinction between children based on status and s 23 gives the unmarried father parental responsibilities and parental rights on almost the same basis as the unmarried mother or married parent. The domicile exception in s 9(1)(a) of the 1986 Act is removed (Sch 3 to the present Act), though the titles of honour exception is retained. Given all of this, the Scottish Parliament considered that the time was ripe to take the final step of abolishing "illegitimacy" as a concept relating to children notwithstanding that the other substantive provisions already mentioned render this step little more than symbolic. But that symbol is important: children are valued by society for themselves and not for the marital (or other) status of their parents. The present section, introduced at Stage 2 as a result of the recommendation of the Justice 1 Committee in its Stage 1 Report, achieves that abolition by amendment to both the title and the content of s 1 of the Law Reform (Parent and Child) (Scotland) Act 1986. Section 1 unambiguously achieves "Abolition of status of illegitimacy" by now providing that no person whose status is governed by Scots law shall be illegitimate. This needs to be read together with s 41 of the present Act, which provides that it is the law of the domicile that determines whether a person's status is affected by the question of whether or not the person's parents are or were married to each other. For a person domiciled in Scotland, that question is not relevant any longer to his or her status.

Consequential amendments are also made, including the repeal in Sch 3 to the Legitimation (Scotland) Act 1968, which had provided a statutory means by which an "illegitimate" child could be "legitimated" through the subsequent marriage of his or her parents, and the repeal of the words "legitimate", "illegitimate" and "legitimacy" in such statutes as the Married Women's Policies of Assurance (Scotland) Act 1880, the Adoption (Scotland) Act 1978 and the Civil Evidence (Scotland) Act 1988. And Sch 2, para 6 adds to s 9 of the Law Reform (Parent and Child) (Scotland) Act 1986 for the avoidance of doubt that s 1 of the 1986 Act applies to adopted children.

22 Domicile of persons under 16

(1) Subsection (2) applies where–
   (a) the parents of a child are domiciled in the same country as each other; and
   (b) the child has a home with a parent or a home (or homes) with both of them.
(2) The child shall be domiciled in the same country as the child's parents.
(3) Where subsection (2) does not apply, the child shall be domiciled in the country with which the child has for the time being the closest connection.
(4) In this section, "child" means a person under 16 years of age.

Before the coming into force of this Act, a child's domicile depended upon whether he or she was "legitimate" or "illegitimate". If the former, he or she took as a domicile that of his or her father; if the latter, the domicile of the mother was conferred upon the child. This was a domicile of dependence since it was traced to the domicile of another person, though since "legitimacy" and "illegitimacy" were determined (by and large) at birth, the first established domicile of a child was also a domicile of origin. No-one ever loses their domicile of origin and, though it might be superseded by the acquisition of a different domicile of dependence or of choice, if a new domicile is subsequently lost before another one is acquired, the domicile of origin revives. Section 21 above has the effect of abolishing the status of "illegitimacy" in Scots law (other than for purposes related to the granting of arms) and it is no longer possible to determine a child's domicile by looking to that status. This section creates a new form of domicile which is at one and the same time a domicile of origin and either a domicile of dependence or an independent domicile. There are two alternatives. First, if the child's parents are domiciled in the same country (which presumably means legal jurisdiction) and the child has his or her home with one or both of the parents, then the domicile of the parents is the child's domicile. If these circumstances exist at the moment of the child's birth (and we need not be too particular about the child "having a home" with his or her parents before leaving the hospital of his or her birth) then that domicile becomes the child's domicile of origin. When the parents change their domicile, the child's domicile changes too: for a domicile of origin in these circumstances is at the same time a domicile of dependence.

This is not a presumption. It is a rule that applies automatically if the circumstances for its application exist. The parents need not share a home, but they must share a domicile and the child must share a home with either one or both of them. The concept of "home" is, perhaps, not so radical an innovation as it appears. It is not a technical concept (as habitual residence might be) but is a matter of fact, closely related to the aims of domicile itself. A child has a "home", it is submitted, where he or she primarily lives and has a centre of gravity. Most children identify with a particular place as their "home" and their perceptions are likely, therefore, to be powerful evidence. The provision accommodates the idea that a child might have more than one home and though it explicitly covers only the situation of the child having two homes, one with each parent, there is nothing to prevent a child from having two homes, one with a parent and one with a non-parental carer (such as a grandparent).

The second alternative is that the facts in subs (1) do not exist. This might be because the parents are not domiciled in the same country, or because one parent has died, or because the child does not have a home with either parent, or because the child was a posthumous child or in some other way has only one parent. In any of these circumstances the rule in subs (2) does not apply to give the child a domicile of dependence, and instead the child's domicile is determined by the quite different rule in subs (3): that the child is domiciled in the country with which he or she has the closest connection. To allow this rule to operate, s 7 of the Age of Legal Capacity (Scotland) Act 1991 has been repealed by Sch 3: that had provided that a child could first obtain an independent domicile on his or her 16th birthday. Now, the "closest connection" test allows an independent domicile to children of any age, so long as the conditions for the application of subs (3) apply. This independently determined domicile will be the child's domicile of origin if the facts in subs (1) do not exist at the time of the child's birth, or it might be a subsequently acquired domicile if, for example, the parents separate after the child's birth and one moves to another country.

The facts in subs (1) are to be determined at the moment at which it is important to determine the child's domicile, as is (where relevant) closest connection, and it follows that a child may move from being governed by subs (2) to subs (3) and back again, depending upon where the parents are domiciled at the relevant time. So for example if a child lives with both parents from birth, he or she takes as a domicile of origin the common domicile of the parents; if the parents (together) move, the child's domicile changes too as a domicile of dependence (but remains governed by subs (2)). But if the parents then separate and one acquires a different domicile from the other then the factual basis for the application of subs (2) no longer exists and the rule in subs (3) takes over. This might not change the child's domicile and in the usual case will not do so, but it might well change the child's domicile in some fairly common circumstances. If the parents are domiciled in, say, England but are temporarily working in Scotland when the child is born, subs (2) will give the child a domicile (of dependence) in England, even when he or she has never been to that country. But if the parents separate and one acquires a domicile other than England, the child's domicile is from that point on determined (independently) by subs (3), based on closest connection, rather than subs (2) – and in the scenario given the child's domicile is likely to become Scotland. And if the parents were to reacquire the same domicile (with or without resuming family life together) and the child continues to live with at least one, subs (2) comes back into play and the child's independent domicile reverts to being a domicile of dependence. Throughout all of this, the child's domicile of origin continues to exist, though it may be in abeyance, waiting to revive if he or she ever loses a domicile before acquiring a new one. But a "closest connection" test will mean that while the person remains a child, the opportunity for the domicile of origin to revive will never present itself: the connection may not be great but there will always be one legal system to which the child is more closely connected than another.

At age 16 the child's domicile becomes one of choice. Though s 7 of the Age of Legal Capacity (Scotland) Act 1991, which gave a child capacity to acquire an independent domicile on his or her 16th birthday, has been repealed, the rules in the present section are explicitly applied only to children under 16. After 16 the young person must be taken to have capacity to change his or her existing domicile, whether that was previously one of dependence or of closest connection, for that is the age at which parents lose the right to regulate the child's residence (Children (Scotland) Act 1995, s 2(7)). It is to be noted that at this stage there is no practical difference between an independent domicile, a domicile of dependence and a domicile of choice. But at 16 the capacity to abandon a domicile before acquiring a new one is acquired and in these circumstances the domicile of origin revives.

There is no definition of the word "parents" given in the Act. Prior to the Act domicile was determined by "legitimacy" or "illegitimacy" and, though this usually also had the effect of determining whether the father had parental responsibilities and parental rights, it was the status of the parental relationship rather than the consequences of that relationship that determined the child's domicile. There is no intention in the present Act to change that proposition, with the result that "parent" must be given its natural meaning and a child's domicile follows the two people whom the law recognises as the child's parents, whether or not they are married to each other and whether or not one or both lacks parental responsibilities and parental rights. This will normally be the genetic parents but might be adoptive parents, parents presumed to be such by the provisions of the Law Reform (Parent and Child) (Scotland) Act 1986 or deemed to be parents by the provisions in the Human Fertilisation and Embryology Act 1990. In any case the law of Scotland recognises no more than two parents and in some limited circumstances only one.

Consequential upon this section is the repeal in Sch 3 of s 4 of the Domicile and Matrimonial Proceedings Act 1973 which made special provision to determine a child's domicile when he or she was not living with his or her father.

23 Parental responsibilities and parental rights of unmarried fathers

(1) Section 3 of the Children (Scotland) Act 1995 (c. 36) (provisions relating both to parental responsibilities and parental rights) shall be amended in accordance with subsections (2) and (3).

(2) In paragraph (b) of subsection (1) (cases in which parents have parental responsibilities and parental rights)–

    (a) the words from "married" to the end shall become subparagraph (i) of that paragraph; and

    (b) at the end there shall be added "or

        (ii) where not married to the mother at that time or subsequently, the father is registered as the child's father under any of the enactments mentioned in subsection (1A).".

(3) After subsection (1) there shall be inserted–

(1A) Those enactments are–

> *(a) section 18(1)(a), (b)(i) and (c) and (2)(b) of the Registration of Births, Deaths and Marriages (Scotland) Act 1965 (c. 49);*
>
> *(b) sections 10(1)(a) to (e) and 10A(1)(a) to (e) of the Births and Deaths Registration Act 1953 (c. 20); and*
>
> *(c) article 14(3)(a) to (e) of the Births and Deaths Registration (Northern Ireland) Order 1976 (S.I. 1976/1041).".*

(4) Paragraph (b)(ii) of subsection (1) of section 3 of the Children (Scotland) Act 1995 (c. 36) (which is inserted by subsection (2)(b)) shall not confer parental responsibilities or parental rights on a man who, before the coming into force of subsections (2) and (3), was registered under any of the enactments mentioned in subsection (1A) of that section (which is inserted by subsection (3)).

When the UK Parliament enacted the Children (Scotland) Act 1995, it did so having accepted all the recommendations of the Scottish Law Commission relating to children contained in its 1992 Report on *Family Law,* other than two proposals: (i) to limit the so-called "right" of parents to assault their children in the name of chastisement (see now s 51 of the Criminal Justice (Scotland) Act 2003); and (ii) to impose parental responsibilities on all parents rather than, as before 1995, only on female parents and married male parents. So in relation to parental responsibilities and parental rights the pre-1995 position survived, notwithstanding its inconsistency with the whole ethos of the Children (Scotland) Act 1995, which is that a parent's relationship with his or her child is primarily one of responsibility rather than of right, and that children should have two adults to look to for protection, advice and guidance and should continue to have two adults to look to even when the adults themselves have separated, and whatever the adults' marital status. The present section deals with this issue, makes the 1995 Act more internally coherent, and at the same time brings Scots law into line with the UN Convention on the Rights of the Child, which prohibits discrimination against children on the basis of their sex or the marital status of their parents. This is one of those issues on which consensus could not be reached in the various consultations that preceded the Bill, though there was a clear preponderance of professional opinion to the effect that the existing situation was not sustainable, given that today in Scotland around 40 per cent of children are born to unmarried parents, the overwhelming majority of whom live together in stable family units.

This provision very substantially ameliorates the position of the unmarried father by amending s 3 of the Children (Scotland) Act 1995, which is the provision that sets out who will have parental responsibilities and parental rights automatically (ie without the intervention of the court). Section 3 now provides that parental responsibilities and parental rights are to be allocated to all mothers and to fathers who are either married to the mother or (the new addition) registered in a birth register in the United Kingdom as father. This will deal with most unmarried fathers, and is likely to include any who have a modicum of relationship with the mother and the child. However, the law still distinguishes to some extent between male and female parents, in at least two respects. First, mothers do not need to register themselves as parents before acquiring parental responsibilities and parental rights. The practical difference will lie with the man who is not registered but who claims to be the father. Obtaining a declarator of paternity has the effect of determining paternity even more securely than registration does (which merely creates a rebuttable presumption, under s 5 of the Law Reform (Parent and Child) (Scotland) Act 1986). But a declarator of paternity does not in itself carry parental responsibilities and parental rights as, now, registration does. In other words, a man who was not presumed father (for whatever reason) but who proves himself in court to be the father will continue to be denied parental responsibilities and parental rights until he has obtained, in addition to the declarator of paternity, an order under s 11 of the Children (Scotland) Act 1995. But while paternity may be a matter of fact, and registration confers parental responsibilities and parental rights automatically without any investigation into welfare, a s 11 order is granted only upon the court being persuaded that it is in the interests of the child that the father be awarded parental responsibilities and parental rights. This is exactly the discriminatory position that held prior to the present Act: parental responsibilities and parental rights follow only a judgement of welfare rather than the fact of parenthood if that fact is established by court declarator rather than presumption or rule of law.

The second difference is between married and unmarried fathers. The new rule confers parental responsibilities and parental rights on the latter if registered in the United Kingdom, but if parental responsibilities and parental rights come from marriage it does not matter where the marriage took place. So parents who married abroad and registered the child abroad will both have parental responsibilities and parental rights, but parents who are not married but registered their child abroad will continue to be treated differently and the father will not have parental responsibilities and parental rights when the family moves here.

And in any case the discrimination against men, the internal inconsistency in the 1995 Act, and the external incompatibility with the UN Convention, will all remain in Scots law for 16 years after the coming into force of the Family Law (Scotland) Act 2006 (ie until May 2022) because subs (4) ensures that the conferral of parental responsibilities and parental rights on unmarried fathers is not retrospective. Most provisions of the present Act will have retrospective effect, but it was felt that parental responsibilities and parental rights should be conferred only on unmarried fathers who are registered as such *after* the Act comes into force (on 4 May 2006). For otherwise fathers who presently have no legitimate say in the upbringing of children already in life would have acquired such a say and it was considered that to allow this would run too great a risk of destabilising existing family relationships. There is some validity to this fear, but it is likely to be realistic in only a minority of families. For the rest, the unmarried father would do well to regularise his situation by acquiring parental responsibilities and parental rights either through a s 4 agreement with the mother (which does not require satisfaction of the welfare test but does require maternal willingness) or by a s 11 order from the court. It is to be noted that subs (4) denies retrospectivity for *registrations* before the Act comes into force, rather than *births*. So if a child is born before the Act comes into force and the father is registered as such after that date, he will acquire automatic parental responsibilities and parental rights.

24 Orders under section 11 of the Children (Scotland) Act 1995: protection from abuse

After subsection (7) of section 11 of the Children (Scotland) Act 1995 (c. 36) (court orders relating to parental responsibilities etc) there shall be inserted–

"(7A) In carrying out the duties imposed by subsection (7)(a) above, the court shall have regard in particular to the matters mentioned in subsection (7B) below.

(7B) Those matters are–

(a) the need to protect the child from–
   (i) any abuse; or
   (ii) the risk of any abuse,
   which affects, or might affect, the child;
(b) the effect such abuse, or the risk of such abuse, might have on the child;
(c) the ability of a person–
   (i) who has carried out abuse which affects or might affect the child; or
   (ii) who might carry out such abuse,
   to care for, or otherwise meet the needs of, the child; and
(d) the effect any abuse, or the risk of any abuse, might have on the carrying out of responsibilities in connection with the welfare of the child by a person who has (or, by virtue of an order under subsection (1), would have) those responsibilities.

(7C) in subsection (7B) above–
  "abuse" includes–
  (a) violence, harassment, threatening conduct and any other conduct giving rise, or likely to give rise, to physical or mental injury, fear, alarm or distress;
  (b) abuse of a person other than the child; and
  (c) domestic abuse;
  "conduct" includes–
  (a) speech; and
  (b) presence in a specified place or area.
(7D) Where–
  (a) the court is considering making an order under sub-section (1) above; and
  (b) in pursuance of the order two or more relevant persons would have to co-operate with one another as respects matters affecting the child,
  the court shall consider whether it would be appropriate to make the order.
(7E) In subsection (7D) above, "relevant person", in relation to a child, means–
  (a) a person having parental responsibilities or parental rights in respect of the child; or
  (b) where a parent of a child does not have parental responsibilities or parental rights in respect of the child, a parent of the child."

Domestic abuse remains the scourge it always has been, destructive of the stability and security that ought to characterise family life, and with effects as deleterious on mental health as on physical wellbeing. The disastrous effects of domestic abuse on children, whether as victims of abuse directed to them or as witnesses of abuse directed to other family members, can hardly be exaggerated. Perhaps worst of all, domestic violence is a learned behaviour and children exposed to it may well, later on, perpetuate the generational cycle (either as adult victims or as perpetrators). Yet as a problem it has remained resistant to attempts to eradicate or even to reduce its incidence. To a large extent this is probably the result of its very nature – domestic, and therefore private; private and therefore hidden from public view. The unpalatable truth is that children are at far greater risk of harm from members of their own families than from strangers. Tampering with the rules of parental responsibilities and parental rights will do virtually nothing to address this serious social problem.

There is little doubt that the courts have long been aware of the destructive potential of domestic abuse and have taken it into account in their decisions over children. The present provision, which imposes an obligation on courts to take it into account, represents a statutory recognition of the seriousness of the problem, but its substantive effect is at the moment unpredictable. Courts might in future hold that the new subsections added to s 11 of the 1995 Act by this section require them to do no more than what they have already been doing; or they might hold that they require them to make explicit mention in their judgments of how the issue of domestic abuse influenced their decision-making; or they might hold that, while not quite a presumption, this new provision represents a legislative expectation that it will be more difficult than previously for those guilty of domestic abuse to be allowed contact with their children.

The technical structure of this provision is that in deciding whether to make an order under s 11 of the 1995 Act, the court has to regard the child's welfare as its paramount consideration and, now, in determining welfare the court is required to have regard in particular to the need to protect the child from abuse or the risk of abuse and to the other related matters listed in the new s 11(7B). "Abuse" is defined widely to include violence and threatening conduct; "conduct" is defined to include speech and simply being in a specified place. The intent is clearly to give the concept of domestic abuse as wide a meaning as possible.

The new s 11(7D) also requires the court whenever it is considering making a s 11 order to consider the appropriateness of the order where its effect would be to require co-operation between two "relevant persons". Though rather clumsily drafted, the meaning of this provision is fairly clear: the court must take account, in determining *whether* to make an order, the likelihood of its efficacy being compromised by lack of co-operation between the parties. Yet it remains obscure how the court is supposed to respond if co-operation is unlikely. A contact order, for example, in favour of a non-resident parent will usually require the co-operation of the resident parent. If the court has determined that it is in the welfare of the child to retain contact with a non-resident parent, that finding is hardly affected by a further finding that the co-operation of the resident parent is unlikely. Lack of co-operation is now to be relevant to the decision of whether to make the order, but the child's welfare remains paramount and is not to be trumped by a finding of likely non-co-operation: a court certainly ought not to refuse to make a contact order in favour of a father which is in the child's welfare just because the mother will not co-operate, for that is giving the resident parent an incentive to refuse co-operation. In the parliamentary debates concern had been frequently expressed at the lack of sanction against a non-co-operating parent and this provision ought not to be interpreted to give that person the ability to argue that his or her non-co-operation should dissuade the court from making an order that is in the child's best interests: the provision was certainly not intended to give one party or the other a veto over any decision the court might otherwise make.

Perhaps all the provision means is that the court should not make an order that will not in practice work, though the "no-order" principle in s 11(7)(a) probably means this in any case.

One distinctly unfortunate feature of this new provision is the use of the phrase "relevant person" to describe those who need to co-operate with each other. Adding this new s 11(7E) into the Children (Scotland) Act 1995 means that the phrase "relevant person" now has three quite separate meanings within that single Act: s 11(7E) for s 11 orders; s 86(4) for parental responsibilities orders; and s 93(2) for children's hearings and related matters.

5 COHABITATION

SECTIONS 25–29 AND 31

Before the coming into force of this Act, the law of Scotland recognised minimal (though some) consequences to the existence of domestic relationships that were not founded upon marriage. Yet for very many years the extent to which couples who live together in conjugal relationships, but who are not married to each other, has been growing in terms of both number and social acceptability. The 2001 Census recorded over 163,000 cohabiting couples in Scotland, which is reported to be an increase in 10 years from 4 per cent of the total number of couples to 7 per cent (*Cohabitation*, SPICe Briefing 05/11, 3 March 2005). The Scottish Law Commission had in 1992 recommended that a number of the consequences currently limited to marriage be extended to cohabiting couples, but without creating a new "status" of cohabiting couple and it is these recommendations that are given effect to here. A balance has to be struck between different imperatives. On the one hand there is the important need to allow people freedom of choice, including the choice of rejecting state regulation of their relationships. This is often particularly desired by individuals who have been married before and who now want to enter into a new domestic relationship while retaining as much control over their own affairs as possible. On the other hand, there is the need to protect the vulnerable, and a desire to give effect to reasonable expectations and to general perceptions of fairness. Domestic relationships, particularly among the heterosexual community, almost invariably involve disparities in earning capacity and economic power, and frequently require for their successful maintenance that one party sacrifice more than the other. The totally hands-off approach to informal domestic relationships that characterised the common law meant that gains and losses were left to rest where they fell. Statute has for almost 30 years given some recognition to cohabitation but the present Act creates far and away the most important financial consequences to unregistered relationships. It seeks a middle way between the two imperatives mentioned above, by creating certain financial claims that can redress the imbalance created or exacerbated by the relationship, but to a much lesser degree than the law provides for married couples or civil partners.

In terms of doctrinal and practical significance, there is no question but that this part of the Family Law (Scotland) Act 2006 overshadows all the others, and that it is for ss 25–29 that this Act will be primarily remembered (and cited). Other sections merely tidy up the law by amending, developing and modernising what is already there, or abolishing old doctrines. The cohabitation provisions, on the other hand, do more than extend the limited rights and responsibilities currently available to cohabitants: they create a whole new basis upon which domestic relationships are conducted and regulated as well as, in s 29, subverting the fundamentally absolutist nature of Scottish succession law. The new rules set out in ss 28 and 29 provide only a skeleton outline of what is being achieved and the Act leaves a large amount of discretion to the court. It is likely to generate a wealth of litigation in the next decade or so. It will be some years before the flesh has been properly put by the courts on the bones designed by the Parliament.

25 Meaning of "cohabitant" in sections 26 to 29

(1) In sections 26 to 29, "cohabitant" means either member of a couple consisting of–
   (a) a man and a woman who are (or were) living together as if they were husband and wife; or
   (b) two persons of the same sex who are (or were) living together as if they were civil partners.

(2) In determining for the purposes of any of sections 26 to 29 whether a person ("A") is a cohabitant of another person ("B"), the court shall have regard to–
   (a) the length of the period during which A and B have been living together (or lived together);
   (b) the nature of their relationship during that period; and
   (c) the nature and extent of any financial arrangements subsisting, or which subsisted, during that period.

(3) In subsection (2) and section 28, "court" means Court of Session or sheriff.

This section attempts to give guidance to the court as to the types of cohabiting couple who are entitled to access the rights and who will be subjected to the liabilities contained in the substantive sections that follow. It was considered insufficient to leave the definition as the bald "living together as husband and wife or as civil partners" and the Parliament is clearly indicating to the courts that the rights and liabilities are to be conferred on stable family units only. Insofar as that message is *not* fully conveyed by subs (1) (for a defining characteristic of married or civilly enpartnered couples is, surely, their stability) the three factors listed in subs (2) attempt to do so but add little in practical terms. It is worth remembering that in some existing statutes where cohabitation is recognised, notably s 18 of the Matrimonial Homes (Family Protection) (Scotland) Act 1981, factors are already listed to assist the court in determining whether two persons are "living together as husband and wife" or (since s 34 of the present Act) "as civil partners" but there has been no case in which the specified factors have been determined (or even discussed). It is virtually impossible to imagine a situation in which a court would hold that a couple *are* living together as husband and wife or as civil partners for the purpose of subs (1) but, because of one of the factors in subs (2), one of them is *not* a "cohabitant" for the purposes of any of the following sections. And, one would imagine, it is entirely impossible for one of a couple to be a cohabitant but the other not. Indeed, it is unlikely that a couple could be considered to be cohabitants for the purposes of this part of this Act but not cohabitants for the purposes of the 1981 Act (or other statutes recognising cohabitation such as the Damages (Scotland) Act 1976). It is submitted therefore that the real *test* is that contained in subs (1) and that subs (2) plays a merely subsidiary role of indicating to the court some, but by no means all, of the factors that will assist it in determining whether that test has been met, without itself creating any hurdles to be crossed additional to that in subs (1) or indeed setting down any determining criteria. Subsection (1) is designed (i) to be as flexible as possible, reflecting the infinite variety of ways in which contemporary families organise their lives together, (ii) to leave it ultimately in the hands of the courts to determine without detailed legislative guidance whether or not a couple may be said to be "cohabiting" and (iii) to ensure that same-sex couples are treated in exactly the same way as opposite-sex couples. Subsection (2) lists those factors that will always be relevant (ie helpful to the court in determining whether the couple are cohabiting) but, given the diverse nature of modern family life, other factors in particular cases may be much more important and even determining.

Subsection (1) uses a familiar formulation which, in truth, has not caused the courts terribly much trouble in the past 30 or 40 years (other than, of late, the now irrelevant question of whether a same-sex couple could be said to be living together as if they were husband and wife). The purpose of this formulation is to confer rights and impose responsibilities upon only those cohabitants who live their lives in a way that is not outwardly distinguishable from the way married couples or civil partners typically live their lives together (other than that the relationship has not been sanctified by the state). The crucial elements to satisfy the test in subs (1) are probably no more than twofold. First, the couple must live together. Of course, there is no legal requirement on married couples or civil partners to live together, but typically most do and an unmarried or unenpartnered couple who do not live together are not following the generality of relationship and are not satisfying the clear words of the statute. Second, the couple's relationship almost certainly must be or have been of a sexual nature. There may well be a doctrinal difference here between marriage and civil partnership, for marriage in the understanding of the law remains explicitly a sexual relationship, with concepts of impotency and adultery retaining legal significance, and (at least according to the House of Lords in *Bellinger* v *Bellinger* [2003] UKHL 21) underpinned by procreative potential. All of this is absent from civil partnership and it is therefore possible (but not desirable) to argue that while a sexual element is necessary before an opposite-sex couple can be said to be "living together as husband and wife" it is *not* necessary before a same-sex couple can be said to be "living together as civil partners". Yet the social expectation is that both types of relationship have a foundation of sexual attraction and, normally, internal sexual activity. The law's conferral of significance on the sexual act in one type of couple but not the other is irrelevant to the determination of whether either type is living *conjugally*. A conjugal relationship has a hint of sex but today a much larger element of companionability and interdependency. In all important (ie non-sexual) matters the aim of the Civil Partnership Act 2004 was to create an institution as similar to marriage as possible, and it follows, it is submitted, that there should be no difference of approach in determining whether a same-sex couple, as opposed to an opposite-sex couple, have satisfied the test in subs (1). It may well be that in practice opposite-sex couples will tend to lead their lives rather differently from same-sex couples and clearly same-sex cohabitants have to be shown to have lived their lives as if they were civil partners rather than as if they were married. But it would be bad social policy to make it more difficult for one or other type of couple to access the important rights and liabilities created by the following four sections of this Act, and there is certainly no evidence of a parliamentary intent to do so.

The indicative elements in subs (2) which the court must take into account in determining the conjugality of the relationship are not defining in the sense that their existence or absence will be conclusive, but they will nearly always assist the court in determining whether or not a cohabitation exists. The specified elements are as follows.

(a) *Length of time the couple have lived together.* It is of course possible that the couple's relationship has lasted significantly longer than their living together, and there is nothing to stop the court taking that into account, in appropriate cases. But the length of time during which the couple have shared accommodation is self-evidently relevant, though there is no minimum period laid down. This is sensible, because of the variety of ways in which people lead their private lives. It also avoids artificial arguments as to when the living together commenced or ended: this will often be gradual in the way that marriage and civil partnership does not start and end gradually but with a single legal act on a specified date. As a general rule, but no more than that, it is likely to be easier to establish a cohabitation after a lengthy period of living together than after a shorter period. If an analogy with marriage by cohabitation with habit and repute is appropriate, the Court of Session was willing to contemplate that a period of just over six months might in some circumstances be sufficient (*Kamperman* v *MacIver* 1994 SLT 763) and it may be that a similar period of time is the minimum before factual living together becomes legal "cohabitation". As a guide, but probably not a rule, this analogy may be useful: it is unlikely that a couple who have shared a home for six weeks will have been able so to meld their lives together in the way that husbands and wives and civil partners do.

(b) *The nature of the relationship during the period the couple lived together.* This is tautologous of the test in subs (1) where living together in a relationship of a particular nature is the very matter at issue – the court is here required to direct its attention to whether the test is satisfied and, as such, subs (2)(b) adds nothing to subs (1).

(c) *The nature and extent of any financial arrangements subsisting during the period the parties lived together.* It is to be noted that the phrase "financial arrangements" is open-ended – it is not limited to such arrangements between the parties. There must, however, be an implicit limitation of relevancy to the question at issue. The financial arrangements must (though the paragraph does not say so) involve at least one of the parties and there must, one assumes, be a connection between the arrangements and the relationship whose nature the court is trying to determine. The fact that, for example, one cohabitant has a subscription to a club or a magazine says nothing about the relationship and can safely be ignored. Financial arrangements between the parties, or between one party and a third party which directly affects the other party to the relationship (eg a tenancy agreement over the house they live in together) will, on the other hand, always be relevant. Any financial *inter*dependency between the parties will be "financial arrangements" that are strongly indicative of living together as husband and wife or as civil partners: this might include holding a joint bank account, taking title to the home in which they cohabit in joint names, or one acting as cautioner to the other for no consideration.

Though the above factors are explicitly listed by the statute as matters always to be taken into account, there is no implication that any other matter is to be ignored. The couple's treatment by friends and family, how they present to the world, whether they are sharing in the upbringing of a child, whether they have a child together, how the child of one relates to or perceives the other, the extent to which they lead their social lives together, and share interests, are all factors that will have some weight and may in particular cases be determining. For all give colour to the relationship between the parties who live together and all, therefore, assist the court in its task of determining whether the test in subs (1) has been satisfied. Some of these factors will be strongly indicative: little if anything more need be shown to establish a cohabitation between a couple who live together and procreate together with the intention of bringing the child up together. But while the presence of these factors indicates cohabitation, their absence should not be taken to indicate the reverse. A couple may choose not to procreate, or to holiday separately, or to keep separate bank accounts and yet to remain a "couple" who live together as husband and wife or as civil partners. Whether the nature of the relationship is such that "family life" can be said to exist between the couple for the purposes of art 8 of the ECHR is another factor that may be important in many cases.

26 Rights in certain household goods

(1) Subsection (2) applies where any question arises (whether during or after the cohabitation) as to the respective rights of ownership of cohabitants in any household goods.

(2) It shall be presumed that each cohabitant has a right to an equal share in household goods acquired (other than by gift or succession from a third party) during the period of cohabitation.

(3) The presumption in subsection (2) shall be rebuttable.

(4) In this section, "household goods" means any goods (including decorative or ornamental goods) kept or used at any time during the cohabitation in any residence in which the cohabitants are (or were) cohabiting for their joint domestic purposes; but this does not include—

(a) money;

(b) securities;

(c) any motor car, caravan or other road vehicle; or

(d) any domestic animal.

This section replicates (though not precisely) the similar rule for married couples and civil partners in s 25 of the Family Law (Scotland) Act 1985 and it serves the same purpose: to provide a means of resolving a dispute as to the ownership of certain goods when proof is absent. Couples, married or enpartnered or simply living together, acquire household goods for the joint purposes of living their lives together and while the relationship lasts ownership between them is seldom relevant or considered. It is a characteristic of marriage and civil partnership (and of couples who live as if they were married or in a civil partnership) that the parties trust each other and so do not keep careful records of who owns what when goods are acquired for use and enjoyment during the relationship. But questions may arise in a variety of circumstances in which the question needs to be answered: such as for example on separation when the parties agree to take away with them their own property but nothing else, on death when the deceased's property is distributed on succession, or on bankruptcy where the creditors can claim the bankrupt's property (but not the property of the bankrupt's partner).

As with marriage and civil partnership, the presumption of common ownership (which, it may be assumed, is what "a right to an equal share" means) applies only to "household goods" as defined in subs (4). Heritable property is excluded because "goods" refers to corporeal moveables. And the presumption applies to goods acquired during the cohabitation, which reflects the marriage and civil partnership rule, though the present provision does not follow the marriage/civil partnership rule in s 25 of the 1985 Act that the equal share presumption also applies to goods "obtained in prospect of ... the marriage or civil partnership". The assumption seems to have been that a couple intending to marry or enter a civil partnership are likely to acquire household goods preparatory to setting up home together while couples intending to cohabit are unlikely to do so. In the generality of cases this may well be right: cohabitations tend to begin with one party moving in with the other rather than, as with marriage at least, both parties moving from the homes they currently occupy to a new, joint, home. (Civil partnership is too new a social institution to state with confidence how it is commonly entered into and for the first few years at any rate that institution will likely be entered into by parties already cohabiting.) However, it is not inconceivable that a couple, planning on setting up a home together, obtain property that will allow them to do so (for example purchasing a bigger bed, to be delivered the day before one moves in with the other): but the presumption will not apply in that situation, though it would if the parties purchased the bed in contemplation of their marriage or civil partnership (and subsequently married or entered a civil partnership).

Much more significant as a difference between this provision and the equivalent s 25 of the 1985 Act, between cohabitants on the one hand and spouses and civil partners on the other, is the omission here of an equivalent to s 25(2). The rule in both provisions is a *presumption,* which can be overturned by any person with an interest showing that the household goods are not, in fact, shared equally. The rule is really designed to deal with the situation in which it is unclear or cannot be established where ownership lies between the parties and it is not needed where clear proof exists. Section 25(2) of the 1985 Act, applicable to spouses and civil partners, strengthens the application of the presumption by providing that it is not to be overturned by showing only that the goods were purchased by either party alone or in unequal shares. There is no equivalent rule for cohabitants, with the result that it may well be sufficient to overturn the presumption for one to prove that he or she purchased the goods alone without a contribution from the other. This difference might well be appropriate, if we remember the fundamental difference between marriage/civil partnership and cohabitation: however stable both forms of conjugal relationship are, the former is bolstered by a joint commitment to (at least attempt to) make it last for life, while there is no such implication with cohabitation. Purchasing household goods while in a relationship without the declaration of commitment to permanency inherent in marriage or civil partnership may rationally be regarded as a more independent act, sufficient in itself to rebut a presumption of sharing of household goods, than the same act in the context of such a commitment. And if goods can be shown to have been purchased jointly, there is no need for the presumption contained in this section. Its effects, therefore, are limited to the situation in which it cannot be proved which of the couple purchased or otherwise acquired the goods in question.

27 Rights in certain money and property

(1) Subsection (2) applies where, in relation to cohabitants, any question arises (whether during or after the cohabitation) as to the right of a cohabitant to–
   (a) money derived from any allowance made by either cohabitant for their joint household expenses or for similar purposes; or
   (b) any property acquired out of such money.
(2) Subject to any agreement between the cohabitants to the contrary, the money or property shall be treated as belonging to each cohabitant in equal shares.
(3) In this section "property" does not include a residence used by the cohabitants as the sole or main residence in which they live (or lived) together.

Again reflecting, though not precisely, the rule applicable to married couples and civil partners in s 26 of the Family Law (Scotland) Act 1985, this section provides that there shall be equal sharing of money or property acquired from savings from a housekeeping allowance that one made to the other. The main difference between the present section and s 26 of the 1985 Act is that the present section explicitly excludes the family home; but since ownership of heritable property will be determined from the title deeds rather than from the source from which the purchase price came, this difference will normally be more apparent than real. However, when the family home is not heritable (for example, a caravan) but was purchased from savings from housekeeping, then the effect of subs (3) is that the caravan belongs to the breadwinner and not the housekeeper, even although it would be jointly owned under s 26 of the 1985 Act if they were spouses or civil partners. Nevertheless, the present section, like s 26 of the 1985 Act, is likely to be a dead letter in modern society in any case: there will be few breadwinners today who make housekeeping allowances to their homemaking partners. Far more commonly, even within cohabitation, the breadwinner's salary will go into a joint bank account to which the partner has access. But if people do arrange their financial affairs in the manner of centuries past, this provision gives some protection to that admirable being, the thrifty housekeeper.

28 Financial provision where cohabitation ends otherwise than by death

(1) Subsection (2) applies where cohabitants cease to cohabit otherwise than by reason of the death of one (or both) of them.

(2) On the application of a cohabitant (the "applicant"), the appropriate court may, after having regard to the matters mentioned in subsection (3)–

    (a) make an order requiring the other cohabitant (the "defender") to pay a capital sum of an amount specified in the order to the applicant;

    (b) make an order requiring the defender to pay such amount as may be specified in the order in respect of any economic burden of caring, after the end of the cohabitation, for a child of whom the cohabitants are the parents;

    (c) make such interim order as it thinks fit.

(3) Those matters are–

    (a) whether (and, if so, to what extent) the defender has derived economic advantage from contributions made by the applicant; and

    (b) whether (and, if so, to what extent) the applicant has suffered economic disadvantage in the interests of–

        (i) the defender; or

        (ii) any relevant child.

(4) In considering whether to make an order under subsection (2)(a), the appropriate court shall have regard to the matters mentioned in subsections (5) and (6).

(5) The first matter is the extent to which any economic advantage derived by the defender from contributions made by the applicant is offset by any economic disadvantage suffered by the defender in the interests of–

    (a) the applicant; or

    (b) any relevant child.

(6) The second matter is the extent to which any economic disadvantage suffered by the applicant in the interests of–

(a) the defender; or

(b) any relevant child,

is offset by any economic advantage the applicant has derived from contributions made by the defender.

(7) In making an order under paragraph (a) or (b) of subsection (2), the appropriate court may specify that the amount shall be payable–

(a) on such date as may be specified;

(b) in instalments

(8) Any application under this section shall be made not later than one year after the day on which the cohabitants cease to cohabit.

(9) In this section–

"appropriate court" means–

(a) where the cohabitants are a man and a woman, the court which would have jurisdiction to hear an action of divorce in relation to them if they were married to each other;

(b) where the cohabitants are of the same sex, the court which would have jurisdiction to hear an action for the dissolution of the civil partnership if they were civil partners of each other;

"child" means a person under 16 years of age;

"contributions" includes indirect and non-financial contributions (and, in particular, any such contribution made by looking after any relevant child or any house in which they cohabited); and

"economic advantage" includes gains in–

(a) capital;

(b) income;

(c) earning capacity;

and "economic disadvantage" shall be construed accordingly.

(10) For the purposes of this section, a child is "relevant" if the child is–

(a) a child of whom the cohabitants are the parents;

(b) a child who is or was accepted by the cohabitants as a child of the family.

Introduction

Without doubt the two most important provisions in this Act are contained in ss 28 and 29, dealing with financial provision between cohabitants on, respectively, separation and death.

Section 28 allows one ex-cohabitant to seek from the court a financial settlement with the other ex-cohabitant within a year of the relationship coming to an end (otherwise than by the death of one or other of them). In many ways this section serves the same function as s 9 of the Family Law (Scotland) Act 1985 but it is, quite deliberately, far more limited than that provision for divorcing spouses or dissolving civil partners. Nevertheless the two possible claims that are open to cohabitants are similar in purpose to the justifications for claiming financial provision on divorce in s 9(1)(b) and (c) of the 1985 Act: equalising imbalances in contributions to the relationship, and sharing future child-care costs. Due to its makeup, the section does not lend itself to easy reading.

Subsection (1) limits claims to situations in which the cohabitants cease to cohabit for some reason other than the death of one or both of them. Usually this will be because the couple have physically separated and are now living at different addresses, but it is possible for a couple to cease to "cohabit" even while continuing to share the same address. Though s 25 does not make this explicit (because it defines the noun "cohabitant" rather than the verb "cohabit") it is submitted that "cease to cohabit" in subs (1) of this section must be read in light of the definition in s 25 so that it means "cease to live together as if the couple were husband and wife or civil partners" rather than simply "cease to live together". If this is so, then a couple who continue to share an address but whose relationship as "a couple" has ended will have "ceased to cohabit" and either may seek an award from the other under this section. For an instructive case involving a married couple where the question of when they had separated was crucial for setting the "relevant date" for the purposes of financial provision, see *Banks* v *Banks* 8 November 2005 (Outer House).

Subsections (2)–(6) describe, though clumsily, the orders that may be made, hint at why they might be made (ie the justification for making them) and set out the factors to be taken into account by the court in considering whether to make an order. The court must have regard to the matters mentioned in subs (3) when making any of the orders listed in subs (2) and, in addition, in considering whether to make the first-mentioned order in subs (2) the court must also have regard to the matters in subss (5) and (6). The test for *whether* to make an order is not differentiated from the consideration of *how much* to award an applicant and it would appear that, though logically these are two separate issues, the court must deal with them as one. The court should not make an award that is too generous or too parsimonious and so the value of the award merges with the question of whether it should be made at all.

Other than the interim order permitted by s 28(2)(c) (whose purpose is self-evidently to make interim arrangements), there are two substantive orders that an applicant can seek and a court may make.

Claim for a balancing lump sum

First, an order under s 28(2)(a) may require the defender to pay a capital sum to the applicant. A "capital sum" does not include an order for the transfer of property, and there is certainly no power for the court to specify from which source the capital sum is to come. The defender's pension fund, for example, is not open for distribution to the applicant unless the defender decides (and is able) to pay the sum due from that source himself.

Section 28(2)(a) itself gives no indication of *why* the court might make this order, and it is necessary to look to the matters that the court has to take into account, listed in subss (3), (5) and (6), to glean the justification. From these matters it can be seen that the purpose of an order under s 28(2)(a) is to redress imbalances in the contributions that each cohabitant made to the relationship, as well as the economic advantages gained through, and the economic disadvantages suffered in the interests of, the relationship. The matters in the relevant subsections overlap to some extent and complement each other but as presented in the Act this is not exactly clear. The matters are as follows:

(i)   the defender's economic advantage derived from contributions made by the applicant (s 28(3)(a));

(ii) the extent to which that advantage is offset by the defender's economic disadvantage suffered in the interests of the applicant or any relevant child (s 28(5));

(iii) the applicant's economic disadvantage suffered in the interests of the defender or any relevant child (s 28(3)(b));

(iv) the extent to which that disadvantage is offset by the applicant's economic advantage derived from contributions made by the defender (s 28(6)).

So the court has to balance the economic advantages derived by either from the contributions of the other, with the economic disadvantages suffered by either in the interests of the other or of any relevant child (defined in subs (10) to mean a child of both and a child accepted by both as a child of their family). The purpose of the order is thus revealed as being to redress any remaining imbalance. If this is so, then no order should be made if the existing advantages and disadvantages are in rough equilibrium. Given the conscious attempt to avoid the language of "justification" (which is the language of financial provision on divorce) this conclusion is one of implication only but, it is submitted, that implication is unavoidable. The truth of the matter is that, notwithstanding the political imperative to avoid replicating the approach of the 1985 Act, this provision is designed to do what s 9(1)(b) of that Act does. Now, s 9(1)(b) has not proved to be a well-used provision but it may well be that the claim under s 28(2)(a), its equivalent for cohabitants, will prove far more popular. For spouses and civil partners the primary claim, applicable in virtually all cases, is for a fair share of matrimonial or partnership property under s 9(1)(a) of the 1985 Act and in most cases this obviates the need to make a s 9(1)(b) claim. But an equivalent of s 9(1)(a) is not available for cohabitants and it is likely that the s 28(2)(a) claim will take on the role of primary claim and that in virtually all cases the applicant will be able to show some remaining imbalance that needs redressing. Another reason why s 28(2)(a) of the present Act may well prove stronger than s 9(1)(b) of the 1985 Act is that the present Act gives much more guidance than the 1985 Act does on what is understood by the balance of "advantages" and "disadvantages". Subsection (9) of the present section explicitly defines "contributions" (in the same way as the word is defined in s 9(2) of the 1985 Act) to include indirect and non-financial contributions and any such contributions made by looking after children of the family or the family home, thereby directing the court to treat these matters as having some economic worth. So a claim might be made by one cohabitant who gave up a job and career and future earning capacity to be a homemaker and child-carer; and it might also be made by a cohabitant who gave up none of these things but nevertheless contributed to the relationship in that way. No method of valuing these contributions and advantages is given in the Act, with the result that the court has no option but to take a "broad brush" approach. Courts should, in order to give the provision teeth, be willing to allocate real value to those factors the Parliament has indicated in subs (9) are within the concepts of "contributions" and "advantages". They are likely to be asked to do so under this provision far more often than at the termination of a marriage or civil partnership.

Claim for a share of future child-care costs

The second substantive order that might be made is structured very differently. The order under s 28(2)(b) does not leave to implication but explicitly specifies in that paragraph itself the reason for making it. Under this paragraph an applicant may seek an order in respect of any economic burden of caring for a child of the cohabitants until the child's 16th birthday: the justification, in other words, is to ensure an appropriate sharing of future child-care costs and as such it serves much the same purpose as s 9(1)(c) of the 1985 Act does for spouses and civil partners. The factors to be taken into account in relation to this order are limited to those specified in subs (3) and the balancing factors in subss (5) and (6) are not relevant. So the defender's economic advantages and the applicant's economic disadvantages are to be considered, but (inexplicably) there is no express requirement to balance them against the defender's disadvantages suffered and the applicant's advantages gained. It is difficult to see how the specified factors in subs (3) will help the court determine whether to make an order under s 28(2)(b) and if so how much, for their relevance to future child-care costs is obscure. The fact that the defender has already derived advantages from the contributions of the applicant does not help in assessing what the applicant now needs in terms of help with future child-care costs: this suggests that "needs" is not in fact the issue. The analogous provision for spouses and civil partners talks of sharing future costs "fairly" between the parties but the present provision does not adopt this straightforward approach and simply requires existing advantages and disadvantages to be taken into account. The only rational interpretation of this most clumsy provision is that the Parliament has left it to the courts to determine the basis upon which an award under s 28(2)(b) is to be valued. A reasonable basis would be one similar to that underlying s 9(1)(c) of the 1985 Act, with "fair" sharing being assessed having regard to the disadvantages the applicant has already suffered and the economic advantages the defender has already gained. But if the court is seeking a "fair" sharing of future child-care costs then the defender's past contributions and the applicant's past economic advantages ought not, it is submitted, to be ignored even in the absence of statutory direction to have regard to them.

Another matter that makes the application of this claim awkward is the fact that the "child" appears in two guises, which must not be confused. The claim itself under s 28(2)(b) is for those future child-care costs that will be borne only for children of whom both cohabitants are the legal parents (whether genetic, or through adoption, or the application of the maternity and paternity rules in the Human Fertilisation and Embryology Act 1990). This is much more limited than the analogous claim under s 9(1)(c) of the 1985 Act for spouses or civil partners, whose claim for future child-care costs can be in respect of any "child of the family", which includes the child of one but not the other. This distinction between the s 9(1)(c) claim and the s 28(2)(b) claim might be justified on the basis that when a person marries or enters into a civil partnership with someone who already has children he or she can be assumed to be taking on an obligation that is expected to last for life, not only towards the spouse or civil partner but to the spouse's or civil partner's children; but when a person simply moves in with another person who already has children, but does not make the life-long commitment inherent in marriage or civil partnership, that assumption cannot be made. An inevitable consequence of this limitation to children of both parties is that the claim may be made by opposite-sex couples but never by same-sex couples (unless, through adoption furth of Scotland, they are both parents)

However, "child" appears in this claim in a second, and wider, guise. For under subs (3) one of the matters to be taken into account in determining whether to make an order in respect of future child-care costs referable to a child of both is the applicant's economic disadvantages suffered in the interests of the defender or "any relevant child". "Relevant child" is defined in subs (10) to include any child accepted by the cohabitants as a child of the family and therefore includes a child of one only. So, rather awkwardly, past disadvantages suffered for child X can be used to determine whether to make an award for the future costs of child Y. For example, Tom and his child Maisie move in with Mary and her child Susan. Tom and Mary subsequently have another child, James. Tom then deserts them all. Mary may make a claim under s 28(2)(b) in respect of James's future costs but not in respect of Susan's or Maisie's. However, in making an order under s 28(2)(b) for James's future costs the court must have regard to Mary's past economic disadvantages suffered in the interests not only of James but also of Susan and Maisie. Again, the extent to which these matters will in practice affect the assessment of a s 28(2)(b) claim is left entirely in the hands of the court.

And there are further anomalies. The drafting of s 28(2)(b) assumes that if a couple have cohabited with a child of one of them but they have now separated, then the child will remain with the parental rather than the non-parental cohabitant. In the generality of cases this might well be so, but it will not be universal practice: in the above example Mary is left looking after Tom's child Maisie and the limitation to claims in respect of a child of both means that she cannot make a claim for a share of Maisie's ongoing child-care costs from Tom, even although Maisie is Tom's own child. Tom's alimentary and child support obligations to Maisie will of course reduce the unfairness, but since he would also have identical obligations to James, in respect of whom Mary can claim extra sums, the unfairness is not completely removed by that route (otherwise the provision would be entirely unnecessary). Secondly, if the limitation of claims to child-care costs of children of both cohabitants is based on the proposition that there was no undertaking of an indefinite obligation to any other child, then it is not justified when just such an obligation is indeed undertaken. In particular, when a couple who are not married or in a civil partnership set out to have a child together, but due to legal definition only one is a parent, it seems unfortunate that on separation the other should not be obliged to continue to contribute to the child's upbringing costs. The typical example would be a female couple who decide to have a child together: only one is the mother and the other is not the parent. Yet they both made a joint decision to bring the child's life into being. On their separation, the resident carer (whichever one it is) can make no claim against the other woman. Had the mother's partner been a man and they had decided to create, through artificial means, a child together, s 28(3) of the Human Fertilisation and Embryology Act 1990 would have turned the man into a "father" and on their separation the mother could make a claim under the present provision because the child would be a child of both. This matter was subject to a proposed amendment at both Stage 2 and Stage 3 as this Bill was being debated but the Executive (and eventually the Parliament) resisted this on the ground that the best solution to the problem would be to amend the 1990 Act (which, being reserved to Westminster, the Scottish Parliament cannot do).

Other matters

Subsection (8) sets a time limit of one year from the cessation of the cohabitation for the making of any claim under s 28. The date of cessation of cohabitation will be a matter of fact to be determined by proof if disputed. See the discussion at p 67 above. Another point worth noting is that there is no equivalent provision to that contained in s 16 of the Family Law (Scotland) Act 1985, which allows the court, in some limited circumstances, to set aside or vary an agreement on financial provision that has been entered into by spouses or civil partners. Cohabitation does not, in other words, reduce the right of the couple to make their own financial arrangements. Or to put the same thought in a negative sense, cohabitants are denied the benefits of protection from entering into contractual relations with their partners even when, due, for example, to imbalances of bargaining power, the agreement is not fair or reasonable.

Finally, it is not outwith the realms of possibility that a claim might be made under this section at around the same time as a different claim is made against the same person under s 8 of the Family Law (Scotland) Act 1985. Spouses and civil partners do not have a preferential claim (as they do in s 29, discussed immediately below) and the existence of concurrent claims, one for the spouse and one for a cohabitant, has an effect only on the resources that are available to meet either. A race to the courthouse will in many cases be advisable, for a claim under either s 8 of the 1985 Act or s 28 of the present Act will not be reduced because there is likely to be a later claim made. There is no procedure to amalgamate the two different claims by two different applicants.

29 Application to court by survivor for provision on intestacy

(1) This section applies where–
   (a) a cohabitant (the "deceased") dies intestate; and
   (b) immediately before the death the deceased was–
       (i) domiciled in Scotland; and
       (ii) cohabiting with another cohabitant (the "survivor").
(2) Subject to subsection (4), on the application of the survivor, the court may–
   (a) after having regard to the matters mentioned in subsection (3), make an order–

      (i) for payment to the survivor out of the deceased's net intestate estate of a capital sum of such amount as may be specified in the order;

      (ii) for transfer to the survivor of such property (whether heritable or moveable) from that estate as may be so specified;

    (b) make such interim order as it thinks fit.

(3) Those matters are–

    (a) the size and nature of the deceased's net intestate estate;

    (b) any benefit received, or to be received, by the survivor–

      (i) on, or in consequence of, the deceased's death; and

      (ii) from somewhere other than the deceased's net intestate estate;

    (c) the nature and extent of any other rights against, or claims on, the deceased's net intestate estate; and

    (d) any other matter the court considers appropriate.

(4) An order or interim order under subsection (2) shall not have the effect of awarding to the survivor an amount which would exceed the amount to which the survivor would have been entitled had the survivor been the spouse or civil partner of the deceased.

(5) An application under this section may be made to–

    (a) the Court of Session;

    (b) a sheriff in the sheriffdom in which the deceased was habitually resident at the date of death;

    (c) if at the date of death it is uncertain in which sheriffdom the deceased was habitually resident, the sheriff at Edinburgh.

(6) Any application under this section shall be made before the expiry of the period of 6 months beginning with the day on which the deceased died.

(7) In making an order under paragraph (a)(i) of subsection (2), the court may specify that the capital sum shall be payable–

    (a) on such date as may be specified;

    (b) in instalments.

(8) In making an order under paragraph (a)(ii) of subsection (2), the court may specify that the transfer shall be effective on such date as may be specified.

(9) If the court makes an order in accordance with subsection (7), it may, on an application by any party having an interest, vary the date or method of payment of the capital sum.

(10) In this section–

"intestate" shall be construed in accordance with section 36(1) of the Succession (Scotland) Act 1964 (c. 41);

"legal rights" has the meaning given by section 36(1) of the Succession (Scotland) Act 1964 (c. 41);

"net intestate estate" means so much of the intestate estate as remains after provision for the satisfaction of–

(a) inheritance tax;

(b) other liabilities of the estate having priority over legal rights and the prior rights of a surviving spouse or surviving civil partner; and

(c) the legal rights, and the prior rights, of any surviving spouse or surviving civil partner; and

"prior rights" has the meaning given by section 36(1) of the Succession (Scotland) Act 1964 (c.41).

In a very real sense, this is the most revolutionary provision in the Act. It is designed to address the long-standing misperception that couples who live together have succession rights in each other's estate, but it does so by subverting the traditional absolutist nature of Scottish succession law. For the first time the court is empowered to exercise a discretion to defeat the rights of those who would take under pre-existing rules on intestacy (contained in the Succession (Scotland) Act 1964) and award part of the estate to a party not mentioned in the 1964 Act. Once the survivor of a couple can show that he or she was a "cohabitant" within the terms of s 25, he or she can ask the court to allocate some or all of the deceased's net intestate estate to the claimant. The court is given little guidance as to when it should accede to this request and less as to how to determine how much to give once it has decided that the cohabitant deserves something. The matter is left very much to the discretion of the court, and one important consequence of that is that the first instance judge's exercise of that discretion will be very difficult to challenge.

Yet the provision is to be welcomed. Not only does it address the misperception mentioned above but it reflects what most people probably think is fair. And in addition it removes the major motivation to claim that there existed a marriage by cohabitation with habit and repute which, in reality, was a means of ameliorating the position of a person who knew well that they had not married but, on the death of their partner, was left shocked to discover that without a will they could claim nothing from the estate. Now, for the first time, a cohabitant will be able to go to court with clean hands, as it were, without having to pretend that the parties had married, and state simply: "As a cohabitant, I should receive something from my dead partner's estate." The provision does not limit itself to claims from those who would otherwise be destitute: it protects not only the vulnerable but also those with reasonable expectations. It aims to do a wider justice than the prevention of serious financial hardship.

However, there are a number of limitations specified in the section as to when the cohabitant may make a claim (in other words, as to the competency of the claim). The first and most crucial one is that the deceased must have died intestate (or at least partially so). Section 29(10) provides that "intestate" is to be construed in accordance with s 36(1) of the Succession (Scotland) Act 1964, which defines "intestate estate" to mean "so much of [the] estate as is undisposed of by testamentary disposition". It follows that while one may not completely disinherit one's spouse or civil partner, one may, by the simple expedient of making a valid and comprehensive will, ensure that one's cohabitant receives nothing from one's estate. Secondly, the deceased must have been, immediately before death, domiciled in Scotland. The normal rules for determining domicile will apply and if the deceased is domiciled according to these rules anywhere other than in Scotland the survivor will not be able to go to the Scottish court under this provision and seek a share of the estate (even if the survivor is domiciled here). This rule is consistent with existing doctrine, for it is the law of the deceased's last domicile that generally governs succession to moveable property. But it should be noted that this section allows the Scottish court to award heritable property as well. In practical terms this will be limited to heritable property in Scotland since the *lex situs* governs succession to immoveable property and a foreign system, if the property is situated abroad, may not recognise or enforce the surviving cohabitant's rights. A third limitation is that the deceased must have been cohabiting with the survivor immediately before death. "Cohabitant" is defined in s 25 by reference both to fact and to nature of relationship. The parties must have been "living together" as a matter of fact, and their relationship must have had certain characteristics (see the discussion of s 25 above). But it is submitted that once the relationship has these characteristics and the parties can be shown to be maintaining their relationship, the courts should not be too assiduous in rejecting claims under this provision because there is doubt as to whether the "living together" condition is satisfied immediately before death. In particular, the fact that one of a couple has lived the last few months or even years of his or her life in long-term nursing care should not remove his or her status as a "cohabitant" if it can be shown that the relationship between the couple continued in the way that one would expect the relationship between married or civilly enpartnered couples in these circumstances would continue. Finally, the claim must be made within six months of the deceased's death. The period is stated to begin with "the day on which the deceased died", which subverts the general rule that the day from which time is to run is excluded from computation of the period (see *B* v *Kennedy* 1992

SLT 870). So if, say, a person dies on 14 February, the claim must be made on or before 13 August. It would be sensible (though often insensitive) for a cohabitant whose partner has disappeared and is thought to be dead to be advised to make a claim as soon as possible and not to wait until the death has been confirmed.

As well as these limitations as to when the claim will be competent, there are other limitations as to how much the court may award a surviving cohabitant when the claim is indeed competent. First, s 29(4) provides a ceiling to what the court may award the survivor: the surviving cohabitant is not ever to receive "an amount" greater than he or she would have received had he or she been married or civilly enpartnered to the deceased. It follows that in every case a calculation will have to be made on the hypothesis that the survivor was indeed a spouse or civil partner. Given the straightforward and non-discretionary nature of the rules of Scottish intestate succession this will not be difficult, but will obviously vary depending upon whether there are children and the extent to which the estate would be eaten up by prior rights. It is to be remembered that in Scotland the majority of intestate estates are smaller than the total figures for prior rights claimable by spouses and civil partners and it follows that it is likely that in most estates the rule in s 29(4) will not, in fact, cut down the amount that a surviving cohabitant can claim – if a spouse or civil partner would have been able to claim the whole estate. Potentially more difficult, however, will be the issue of valuation. Section 29(2)(a)(ii) allows the court to make a property transfer order but that must not be "an amount" in excess of what a spouse or civil partner would have received. The date of valuation is, it may be assumed, the date of death but the method of valuation is not set out in the Act. It may be that the court will adopt a similar approach to valuation to that adopted in relation to financial provision on divorce.

Secondly, the surviving cohabitant's claim may be made only against the "net intestate estate", which is defined in s 29(10) to be that part of the estate remaining after the satisfaction of inheritance tax, any other liability which has priority over legal rights and prior rights and, if the cohabitant died while still married or in a civil partnership, any claim for either legal rights or prior rights that their surviving spouse or civil partner has. This definition is of crucial importance in setting where the surviving cohabitant's claim comes in the ranking of claims against an estate. As always, external liabilities of the estate come first. Then, if the deceased, while cohabiting with the survivor, remained at the date of his or her death married or civilly enpartnered, the claims of the spouse or civil partner come next, though only to the extent of their prior and legal rights. Once these have been satisfied, it is here that the surviving cohabitant's claim fits in: a s 29 claim can be made over anything that is left, and that claim will have priority over any claim by descendants to legal rights and to the free estate under s 2 of the Succession (Scotland) Act 1964, claims by ascendants, siblings and even any surviving spouse or civil partner to the free estate under s 2.

In any case, whenever the court makes an award to a surviving cohabitant under this provision, those who would otherwise succeed will lose out. If the deceased is survived by children, they will now rank below the cohabitant and their legal rights will be calculated after the cohabitant's claim has been determined. However, the executor will never know the value of the cohabitant's claim because, uniquely, this lies in the discretion of the court. It follows that whenever there is a person who might be a cohabitant, an executor will not be able to calculate the shares of any other claimant until (i) the potential cohabitant has made a claim and (ii) that claim has been determined by the court.

The court is given little guidance as to how to assess the claim that is made but is required, in doing so, to take account of the factors in subs (3), as follows:

(i) *The size and nature of the deceased's net intestate estate.* The court will always need to know the size of the net estate because it is a capital sum or a transfer of property that can be ordered rather than a percentage of the estate. The nature of the estate is also important because the court will need to know how realisable the assets are before determining whether a capital sum or a property transfer order is more apt. And the court may well be less inclined to award a transfer of property if it has heirloom value, or to award a lump sum that would have the effect of compromising a family business.

(ii) *Any benefit the survivor will receive in consequence of the death.* This might be an insurance payout, or compensation under the Damages (Scotland) Act 1976, made to the survivor that has the effect of ameliorating the injustice this provision is designed to address.

(iii) *The nature and extent of other claims on the estate.* This directs the court's attention to the question of who loses out if the surviving cohabitant is awarded anything. A surviving spouse's or civil partner's claims to prior and legal right are not relevant here (they are already taken into account in determining the net intestate estate). What the court has to do at this stage is to take account of claims lower down the ranking, such as legitim and the s 2 rights that might inhere in surviving spouses, civil partners, children, parents or siblings. The aim of the court is to determine who, in justice, should receive what, and it is here that is located the most open-ended element of the court's discretion. Section 29 does not say so explicitly but what the court is surely aiming for is to strike a just and equitable balance between the expectations and needs of the surviving cohabitant and those who will lose out if any award is made under this provision. It will be for the higher courts, in the fullness of time, to lay down which sorts of factors are significant in this process but they may well decide that affection and distance of relationship between the deceased and the competing claimants, who took care of the deceased, and even other claimants' relationship with the surviving cohabitant are all relevant. The courts may well decide to start with a presumption that, once a surviving cohabitant has shown him or herself to be a "cohabitant", they should receive exactly what a spouse or civil partner would have received, the onus being on the competing claimants to show why this is unfair or too generous. Then again, the courts might determine that no presumptions are appropriate here. At this early stage all that can be said is that a lengthy period of uncertainty is likely, and that the only stability is the high probability that cohabitants will invariably claim the maximum they might receive under this provision. If there are no other claimants at all, the competing claim is that of the Crown, but it may safely be assumed that a cohabitant's claim will always be regarded as stronger than that of the Crown as *ultimus haeres*.

(iv) *Any other matter the court considers appropriate.*

Though the provision is worded in terms of "the survivor" making the claim and the purpose of the provision is to give "the survivor" some direct benefit, it is arguable that this phrase should be interpreted to include the survivor's representatives. Clearly this will be possible if the survivor raises an action under s 29 but dies before its completion – his or her executor will be able to complete the action. Similarly, a representative will be able to make a s 29 application if the survivor is incompetent (but alive). It is less clear that if no application is made during the survivor's life his or her executor can instigate it after his or her death on behalf of the survivor's successors. Imagine the following scenario. A wealthy man cohabits with a woman and her (but not his) child. The cohabitants are both killed in a car crash and, the man being younger, it is presumed that he died first under s 31(1)(b) of the Succession (Scotland) Act 1964. (That statute is not amended at all by the present Act, but its operation is significantly affected and a s 29 claim is clearly a "purpose affecting ... succession to property" which activates the common calamity rule in s 31.) Is the child to be left without a claim against the estate of his mother's cohabitant, or can his mother's executor raise the action under this section that she could have raised had she lived long enough? Justice, it is submitted, points to the latter conclusion and this can be achieved by interpreting "the survivor" to include the survivor's representatives. If the woman died first (which might be established by no more than proof of her age) then there would be no survivor's claim against the man's estate to transmit to the woman's successor.

31 Domestic interdicts

(1) The 1981 Act shall be amended in accordance with subsections (2) and (3).

(2) In subsection (3) of section 18 (cohabiting couples: occupancy rights and application of certain provisions of Act), for the words from "sections", where it first occurs, to "17" there shall be substituted "section 13".

(3) After section 18 there shall be inserted–
        "Domestic interdicts"

"18A Meaning of "domestic interdict"

(1) In section 18B, "domestic interdict" means–

    (a) an interdict granted on the application of a person ("A") who is (or was) living with another person ("B") as if they were husband and wife against B for any of the purposes mentioned in subsection (2); or

    (b) an interdict granted on the application of a person ("C") who is (or was) living with another person ("D") as if they were civil partners against D for any of the purposes mentioned in subsection (2).

(2) Those purposes are–

    (a) restraining or prohibiting such conduct of the defender towards–

      (i) the pursuer; or

      (ii) any child in the permanent or temporary care of the pursuer,

    as the court may specify;

    (b) prohibiting the defender from entering or remaining in–

      (i) a family home occupied by the pursuer and the defender;

      (ii) any other residence occupied by the pursuer;

      (iii) any place of work of the pursuer;

      (iv) any school attended by a child in the permanent or temporary care of the pursuer.

(3) In this section and in section 18B–

"family home" means, subject to subsection (4), any house, caravan, houseboat or other structure which has been provided or has been made available by the pursuer or the defender (or both of them) as (or has become) a family residence for them and includes any garden or other ground or building usually occupied with, or otherwise required for the amenity or convenience of, *the house, caravan, houseboat or other structure; but does not include a residence provided or made available by any person for the pursuer or, as the case may be, the defender to reside in (whether or not with any child of the pursuer and the defender) separately from the defender or, as the case may be, the pursuer; and*

"interdict" includes interim interdict.

(4) *If the tenancy of a family home is transferred from a pursuer to a defender (or, as the case may be, from a defender to a pursuer) by agreement or under any enactment, the home shall, on such transfer, cease to be a family home.*

(5) *In subsection (3), "child of the pursuer and the defender" includes any child or grandchild of the pursuer or the defender, and any person who has been brought up or treated by the pursuer or the defender as if the person were a child of the pursuer or, as the case may be, the defender, whatever the age of such a child, grandchild or person.*

18B Domestic interdicts: further provision

(1) *Subsection (2) applies if the defender–*
   (a) *is entitled to occupy a family home;*
   (b) *is permitted by a third party to occupy it; or*
   (c) *has, by virtue of section 18(1), occupancy rights in it.*
(2) *Except where subsection (3) applies, the court may not grant a domestic interdict prohibiting the defender from entering or remaining in the family home.*
(3) *This subsection applies if–*
   (a) *the interdict is ancillary to an exclusion order; or*
   (b) *an order under section 18(1) granting or extending occupancy rights is recalled."*

One of the most socially startling aspects of the 1981 Act as originally passed was that it explicitly extended many of its provisions to (opposite-sex) cohabiting couples: at that time this was a radical departure from the law's traditional hands-off approach to unmarried relationships. Crucially, cohabitants could access the provisions relating to "matrimonial interdicts" (ss 14–17), though there were a number of clumsy rules to ensure that the interdict obtained by a cohabitant was not entitled "matrimonial". The original 1981 definition of "cohabitant" was explicitly gender-specific with the result that, even after the passing of the Human Rights Act 1998, it was not possible to interpret it to include same-sex cohabitants. The amendments contained in the present section are designed to separate out "matrimonial interdicts" from those available to cohabitants and also to allow same-sex cohabitants access to the protections interdicts provide. So the extension in s 18(3) of the "matrimonial interdict" provisions in ss 14–17 to cohabitants is repealed and replaced with new sections 18A and 18B. These create the new concept of "domestic interdicts" which apply directly to cohabitants, of whatever gender mix, rather than cohabitants having extended to them the provisions available to married couples or civil partners.

The cleaner result is that spouses will have access to "matrimonial interdicts" under s 14 of the 1981 Act; civil partners will have access to "relevant interdicts" under s 113 of the Civil Partnership Act 2004; and, now, cohabitants of either gender mix will have access to "domestic interdicts" under the new ss 18A and 18B of the 1981 Act and the commentary to ss 10 and 32 in Chapter 2 should be referred to for details relevant to all these forms of family interdict (to coin a generic phrase). There is no substantive difference between any of these forms of interdict, other than that powers of arrest attached to them under the Protection from Abuse (Scotland) Act 2001 *must* be attached in relation to matrimonial interdicts and relevant interdicts but in relation to domestic interdicts for cohabitants the court must do so only if the conditions in s 1(2) of the 2001 Act have been satisfied, that is to say the interdicted person has been given the opportunity of being heard and the power of arrest is necessary to protect the applicant from abuse in breach of the interdict.

6 CIVIL PARTNERS AND SAME-SEX COHABITANTS

SECTIONS 30 AND 33–36; SCH 1, PARA 3; SCH 2, PARAS 2 AND 7–8

The Civil Partnership Act 2004, though passed by the Westminster Parliament, contained provisions applying to Scotland notwithstanding that family law is one of the central areas devolved to the Scottish Parliament. That body had decided to permit Westminster to legislate on its behalf in this area and gave effect to that decision by the process of a "Sewel Motion". Given that the civil service in London no longer takes the care it did in pre-devolution days to get Scottish legislation right, it is no surprise that many errors appeared in the Scottish parts of the 2004 Act. Some of these errors were rectified by Regulations, made under s 259(1)–(3) of the 2004 Act, such as the Civil Partnership Act 2004 (Consequential Amendments) (Scotland) Order 2005, SSI 2005/623, which came into force on 5 December 2005, the same day as the Civil Partnership Act 2004 itself came into force. This Order amends various existing statutes, such as the Human Tissue Act 1961, the Land Registration (Scotland) Act 1979, the Anatomy Act 1984, the Mortgage Rights (Scotland) Act 2001 and the Land Reform (Scotland) Act 2003, usually by inserting "or civil partner" after the various uses of the word "spouse" in these statutes. The most substantive amendment made by these Regulations was to Sch 1 to the Marriage (Scotland) Act 1977, which lists the relationships of affinity within which marriage is permitted only in limited circumstances. The 2004 Act had prohibited a person from entering into a civil partnership with the former spouse of his or her parent, or with the former civil partner of his or her parent; the 1977 Act already prohibited a person from entering into a marriage with the former spouse of his or her parent. But neither Act prohibited a person from entering into a marriage with a former civil partner of his or her parent. The new para 2 of Sch 1 to the 1977 Act, as substituted by the 2005 Order, makes the appropriate prohibition. Other regulations amend various UK statutes, originally forgotten about: see, for example, the Civil Partnership Act 2004 (International Immunities and Privileges, Companies and Adoption) Order 2005, SI 2005/3542. And other primary legislation other than the present Act has rectified (or is rectifying) errors: so, for example, the Local Electoral Administration and Registration Services (Scotland) Bill 2006 introduces a new s 95A into the 2004 Act, replicating s 23A of the Marriage (Scotland) Act 1977 (procedural errors may be ignored) which had originally (and wrongly) been deemed unnecessary for civil partners.

Other amendments to the Civil Partnership Act 2004 have been made necessary in order to replicate the new marriage provisions contained in the present Act. And at least one provision (the repeal in Sch 3 to the present Act of the Law Reform (Husband and Wife) Act 1962), though limited to marriage, has the effect, by its removal from the law, of removing an unnecessary distinction between marriage and civil partnership. Another repeal contained in Sch 3 is of s 129 of the Civil Partnership Act 2004 and its marriage equivalent, s 19 of the Court of Session Act 1988. These provisions allowed the Lord Advocate to intervene in actions for divorce or dissolution in the public interest, and they are now repealed on the basis that there is seldom if ever a public interest in individual marriages or civil partnerships (as opposed to these institutions themselves). Schedule 2 to the present Act also corrects an omission to the 2004 Act's amending of the Family Law (Scotland) Act 1985. Section 16(1) and (3) of the 1985 Act, dealing with agreements on financial provision, were re-worded in 2004 to include dissolution of civil partnership, but s 16(2) was not. That omission is rectified in para 5(3) of Sch 2.

Same-sex cohabitants are fully included in the present Act, which also makes important amendments to provisions relating to cohabitants contained in other legislation. The Civil Partnership Act 2004 was not originally designed to deal with same-sex cohabitants and, though some provisions in that Act did so, there was no comprehensive extension of existing cohabitants' rights to same-sex couples. The Scottish Parliament, since its re-establishment, has been admirably punctillious in ensuring that whenever family rights and responsibilities are enacted, same-sex couples are included, but there remained even after 2004 numerous pre-devolution Acts of the UK Parliament that dealt with cohabitants but did not originally extend to same-sex couples. So the opportunity has been taken with the Family Law (Scotland) Act 2006 to extend existing cohabitants' rights to same-sex cohabitants. Most, but not all, of the amendments to the Civil Partnership Act are contained in the schedules, while most (but not all) of the amendments to cohabitation provisions are contained in the body of the Act.

30 Administration of Justice Act 1982: extension of definition of "relative"

In section 13 of the Administration of Justice Act 1982 (c. 53) (supplementary provisions and definitions in relation to Part 2), in the definition of relative, after paragraph (b) insert–

> *"(ba) any person not being the civil partner of the injured person, who was, at the time of the act or omission giving*

rise to liability in the responsible person, living with the injured person as the civil partner of the injured person".

The Administration of Justice Act 1982 was one of the earliest private law statutes to give explicit recognition to unmarried couples. It provides that when a person is injured as a result of a wrongful act or omission, any "relative" to whom the injured party provided services can sue for the loss of these services due to the injury; "relative" was originally defined in s 13 of the 1982 Act to include both spouse and person living with the injured party as if they were husband and wife (ie opposite-sex cohabitant). The Civil Partnership Act 2004 (Sch 28, para 47) extended the definition of "relative" to include civil partners but it did not extend the definition to include same-sex cohabitants (notwithstanding that the equivalent amendments to the Damages (Scotland) Act 1976 included them). This omission is filled by this section and "relative" in the 1982 Act now includes married couples, opposite-sex cohabitants, civil partners, and same-sex cohabitants.

33 Amendments of Civil Partnership Act 2004

Schedule 1, which contains amendments to the Civil Partnership Act 2004 (c. 33) shall have effect.

Many amendments to the 2004 Act beyond those simply forgotten about or ignored when that Act was passed have been required in order to replicate the amendments to the marriage and divorce laws contained in the present Act. Most are contained in Sch 1 and are dealt with in their appropriate places throughout this commentary.

The only substantive amendment to the Civil Partnership Act 2004 not mentioned elsewhere is the following.

Schedule 1, para 3: Amendments of the Civil Partnership Act 2004

...

> *(b) in subsection 7 [of section 101 of the 2004 Act: right of civil partner without title to occupy family home]*
>> *(i)   in the definition of "child of the family", for the words from "a", where it first occurs, to "family", there shall be substituted "any child or grandchild of either civil partner, and any person who has been brought up or treated by either civil partner as if the person were a child of that partner, whatever the age of the child, grandchild or person"; and*
>> *(ii) in the definition of "family", for "so accepted" there shall be substituted ", grandchild or person so treated".*

Occupancy rights in the Matrimonial Homes (Family Protection) (Scotland) Act 1981 confer on spouses the right to occupy the matrimonial home together with any "child of the family" which is defined in s 22 of that Act relationally and to include both grandchildren and persons "treated" as children of the family. For some reason the Civil Partnership Act 2004, when it replicated the rules for occupancy rights for civil partners, defined "child of the family" in s 101(7) as originally passed in much more limited terms. It defined "child" in terms of age rather than relationally, excluded grandchildren, and instead of "children treated" as members of the family referred to "children accepted". Now, "treated" and "accepted" are different concepts: acceptance is a mental process while treatment is a physical activity and so easier to prove: acceptance can be done before the birth of the child while treatment cannot be. The end result was that fewer children being brought up by (same-sex) civil partners enjoyed protection from domestic violence and occupancy rights than children being brought up by (opposite-sex) spouses. A non-entitled spouse exercising occupancy rights could continue to live in the matrimonial home with her (say) 19-year-old daughter and 1-year-old grandchild; but a non-entitled civil partner seeking to exercise occupancy rights could do so only with her own children under the age of 16, and any child over that age, or grandchild of any age, could be expelled by the entitled civil partner. Perhaps Westminster thought that gay and lesbian people would not be as nasty to each other as heterosexual people. The Scottish Parliament did not take this rosy view of same-sex relationships and this provision (introduced into the Act as one of the very few non-Executive amendments to be accepted) removes the original definition of "child of the family" and substitutes one on all fours with that in the 1981 Act applicable to married couples.

34 Application of 1981 Act to cohabiting couples of same sex

(1) Section 18 of the 1981 Act (occupancy rights of cohabiting couples) shall be amended in accordance with subsections (2) and (3).

(2) In subsection (1)–

    (a) after "wife" there shall be inserted "or two persons of the same sex are living together as if they were civil partners"

    (b) after "wife (", there shall be inserted "in either case"; and

    (c) for "man and the woman" there shall be substituted entitled partner and the non-entitled partner".

(3) In subsection (2)–

    (a) for "a man and a woman" there shall be substituted "two persons"; and

*(b) in paragraph (b), for the words from "are" to the end of
that paragraph there shall be substituted "is any child–*
(i)   of whom they are the parents; or
(ii) who they have treated as a child of theirs.".

The Matrimonial Homes (Family Protection) (Scotland) Act 1981
was a revolutionary piece of legislation, providing new preventive
measures and remedies for domestic violence, and conferring
rights of occupancy in the "matrimonial home" on the spouse of the
home-owner (see Chapter 2).

Another (at the time) startling feature of the legislation was that
it extended many (but not all) of the rights and responsibilities
contained in the Act to unmarried cohabiting couples – that is to say
couples who lived together as if they were husband and wife. The
definition of a "cohabiting couple" is contained in s 18 of the 1981 Act
and it originally referred to "a man and a woman ... living with each
other as if they were man and wife". Sometimes, phrases that refer
to couples living together as if they were husband and wife have
been interpreted to include same-sex couples (see *Ghaidan* v *Godin-
Mendoza* [2004] UKHL 30). But it was not possible to interpret s 18 in
this way because of the reference to "a man and a woman". The Civil
Partnership Act 2004 created similar rights for civil partners as the
1981 Act confers on spouses, but it failed to extend the cohabitants'
rights in the 1981 Act to same-sex couples who had not registered
their relationship as a civil partnership. The present section fills that
gap, by extending the definition of a "cohabiting couple" in the 1981
Act to include two persons of the same sex who are living together
as if they were civil partners. In determining whether a couple are
"cohabiting" the court must take into account not only the length
of time the couple have been living together (s 18(2)(a)) but also
whether there is a child (i) of whom they are the parents or (ii) who
they have treated as a child of theirs. The existence of any child is
not determinative, but it will go some way to indicate the nature
of the relationship between the couple. A child "treated as a child
of theirs" might include a child of one but not the other and even
a child of neither: this will be the common scenario for same-sex
couples. It is, however, to be remembered that it is already possible
for a same-sex couple both to be the legal parents of a child. Such
couples are entitled to adopt a child together in many legal systems,
including England and Wales, and if they do so and the adoption is
recognised here (as it must be if granted by a court in England and
Wales – Adoption (Scotland) Act 1978, s 38(1)(c)), they will be treated
in Scotland as both being parents of the child.

It is to be remembered that the definition of "cohabiting couple"
for the purposes of the 1981 Act is to be found in the amended s 18
thereto and not in s 25 of the present Act (which provides a rather
different definition for the purposes of the substantive rights in
ss 26–29). However, any difference between the two definitions is

unlikely to have any practical effect in determining which couples can access the rights contained in either the 1981 Act or the present Act, for reasons elaborated in the commentary to s 25 in Chapter 5 .

35 Amendments of Damages (Scotland) Act 1976

(1) The Damages (Scotland) Act 1976 (c. 13) shall be amended in accordance with subsections (2) to (5).

(2) In subsection (4) of section 1 (rights of relatives of deceased person), at the beginning there shall be inserted "Subject to subsection (4A),".

(3) After that subsection, there shall be inserted–

"(4A) Notwithstanding section 10(2) of, and Schedule 1 to, this Act, no award of damages under subsection (4) above shall be made to a person related by affinity to the deceased.

(4B) In subsection (4A), a "person related by affinity to the deceased" includes–

    (a) a stepchild, step-parent, stepbrother or stepsister of the deceased; and

    (b) any person who was an ascendant or descendant of any of the step-relatives mentioned in paragraph (a).".

(4) In subsection (2) of section 10 (interpretation), for the words from "sub-paragraph" to "or (c)", there shall be substituted "any of sub-paragraphs (a) to (cc)".

(5) In paragraph 1 of Schedule 1 (definition of relative)

    (a) in sub-paragraph (c), for "paragraph" there shall be substituted "sub-paragraph";

    (b) after that sub-paragraph, there shall be inserted–

"(ca) any person not falling within subparagraph (b) above who accepted the deceased as a child of the person's family;

(cb) any person who–

    (i)   was the brother or sister of the deceased; or

    (ii) was brought up in the same household as the deceased and who was accepted as a child of the family in which the deceased was a child;

(cc) any person who was a grandparent or grandchild of the deceased;";

    (c) in sub-paragraph (d), after "person" there shall be inserted "not falling within sub-paragraph (b) or (cc) above"; and

    (d) in sub-paragraph (e), after "person" there shall be inserted "not falling within sub-paragraph (cb)(i) above".

The Damages (Scotland) Act 1976 allows members of a deceased's family to sue for damages if the deceased had been killed as a result of a delict. Damages may be claimed for either patrimonial or non-patrimonial loss (that is to say economic loss such as loss of the financial support provided by the deceased, or personal hurt such as distress at the deceased's suffering and grief at the death). Different members of the family can sue depending upon which form of loss is claimed, with a longer list of relatives being able to sue for patrimonial loss, and a rather shorter list of relatives being able to sue for non-patrimonial loss. The Scottish Law Commission issued a discussion paper on *Title to Sue for Non-Patrimonial Loss* in 2001 (Scot Law Com DP No 116), and then made recommendations in its Report which was published in 2002 (Scot Law Com No 187). This provision deals with the issues the Scottish Law Commission identified, and gives effect to all its recommendations.

The "immediate family" who were, prior to the present amendments, able to sue for non-patrimonial loss arising from the death of a family member were listed in s 10(2) of the 1976 Act, being spouse, opposite-sex cohabitant, child and parent. *Ghaidan* v *Godin-Mendoza* [2004] UKHL 30 may well have required the definition of "cohabitant" to be extended to same-sex cohabitants (see *Telfer* v *Kellock* 2004 SLT 1290), but in any case the Civil Partnership Act 2004 brought both civil partners and same-sex cohabitants within the terms of the 1976 Act (though it did so in a flawed manner, necessitating the further amendments in Sch 2, para 2 discussed later in this chapter). These categories of "immediate family" were extended, perhaps outwith their obvious or natural meaning, by para 2 of Sch 2 to the 1976 Act which provided that relationships of affinity were to be treated in the same way as relationships of consanguinity (so for example the deceased's mother-in-law had the same right to sue as the deceased's own mother: see *Monteith* v *Cape Insulation* 1998 SC 903); that half-blood relationships were treated as full-blood relationships; and that step-children were treated in the same way as natural children. The Scottish Law Commission felt that in these respects the definition of "immediate family" was unnecessarily wide. And in other respects the definition was considered unnecessarily narrow, for example in its omission of grandparents and, in particular, of siblings and of same-sex cohabitants. The common law had provided no remedy to siblings but even before the 1976 Act the Court of Session in *McKendrick* v *Sinclair* 1972 SC (HL) 25 called for legislative change, though the 1976 Act did not pay heed to that call. The present Act finally does so.

Subsection (3) of the present section excludes affinitive relations as such (including step-relations) from claims for non-patrimonial loss, though they will still be able to claim for patrimonial loss under s 1(3) of the 1976 Act. Indeed, affinitive relations who, by reason other than affinity, come within a specified category (typically, having accepted, or been accepted, as a child of the family) can sue for non-patrimonial loss. This was certainly the intention of the Scottish Law Commission (see para 2.39 of Scot Law Com No 187) and though the new s 1(4A) superficially reads as an absolute bar on affinitive claimants, that strict interpretation must be rejected. For otherwise cohabitants who accept each other's children as children of their family would have a claim while spouses and civil partners who did so would not. Not only is this highly unlikely to reflect parliamentary intention, but it satisfies no legitimate aim. As such it is permitted, even necessary, for the court to read into the new s 1(4A) of the 1976 Act words such as "solely on the basis of the affinity".

Subsection (5) adds new categories of relative to the list of "immediate family" entitled to claim damages for non-patrimonial loss. These are as follows:

(1) *Siblings.* This resolves the flaw identified by the Court of Session in 1972 in *McKendrick* v *Sinclair.*

(2) *Grandparents and grandchildren* (but no further in the ascending or descending line).

(3) *Persons who accepted the deceased as a child of their family.* This irons out a little crease in the previous law that while a child accepted by the deceased as a member of his or her family could sue on the death of the deceased, the accepting adult could not sue on the death of the child. This includes (but is not limited to) step-relationships and to cohabitation equivalents.

(4) *Persons who were brought up in the same household as the deceased and who were accepted as a child of the family in which the deceased was a child.* Typically this will be a step-sibling but it will also include persons brought up by cohabiting couples (opposite-sex or same-sex) together with children with whom they have no formal legal relationship.

The Scottish Law Commission recommendation to include same-sex cohabitants within the definition of "immediate family" was given effect to in the Civil Partnership Act 2004, but the provision that did so was flawed and was never brought into effect. It was replaced by the provision in Sch 2 considered immediately below.

Schedule 2, para 2: Minor and consequential amendments

The Damages (Scotland) Act 1976 (c. 13)
(1) In paragraph 1 of Schedule 1 to the Damages (Scotland) Act 1976 (definition of "relative")–
(a) in sub-paragraph (a), after "spouse" there shall be inserted "or civil partner";

(b) in sub-paragraph (aa)–
  (i) after "spouse" there shall be inserted "or civil partner"; and
  (ii) at the end there shall be added "or in a relationship which had the characteristics of the relationship between civil partners";
(c) after sub-paragraph (e), the word "and" shall be repealed; and
(d) after sub-paragraph (f), there shall be added "and (g) any person who, having been a civil partner of the deceased, had ceased to be so by virtue of the dissolution of the civil partnership.".

The Civil Partnership Act 2004 attempted to bring both civil partners and same-sex cohabitants within the terms of the Damages (Scotland) Act 1976, allowing them to claim damages for both patrimonial and non-patrimonial loss. The amendment in the 2004 Act (Sch 28, para 42) did so ineptly, by amending the wrong sub-paragraph in Sch 1 to the 1976 Act. This provision corrects that error and so civil partners and same-sex cohabitants are now included within the definition of "immediate family" entitled to sue for both patrimonial and non-patrimonial loss on the wrongfully caused death of their partner. The very last provision here allows an ex-civil partner to seek damages for patrimonial loss on the death of their ex-partner after the relationship has been brought to a legal end by dissolution. This replicates the position for spouses and is designed to recognise that an arrangement on divorce or dissolution might well involve one ex-partner taking on continuing financial obligations to the other, which would be destroyed by the untimely death of the obligant.

36 Amendments of Adults with Incapacity (Scotland) Act 2000

Section 24 of the Adults with Incapacity (Scotland) Act 2000 (asp 4) (termination of continuing or welfare power of attorney) shall be amended as follows–

(a) after subsection (1) there shall be inserted–
  "(1A) If the granter and the continuing or welfare attorney are in civil partnership with each other the power of attorney shall,unless the document conferring it provides otherwise, come to an end on the granting of–
    (a) a decree of separation of the partners in the civil part-nership;
    (b) a decree of dissolution of the civil partnership;
    (c) a declarator of nullity of the civil partnership.";
(b) in subsection (4), after "(1)" there shall be inserted "or subsection (1A)".

This is another provision that ought to have appeared in the Civil Partnership Act 2004 in order to ensure that civil partnership and its dissolution have the same effects as marriage and divorce. Section 24(1) of the Adults with Incapacity (Scotland) Act 2000 provides that one of the consequences of divorce (or decree of separation or nullity) is to terminate any continuing or welfare power of attorney accepted under the terms of that Act between spouses. The same result now follows when a civil partnership is dissolved or there is a decree of separation or nullity.

Schedule 2, para 7: Minor and consequential amendments

In subsection (7) of section 1 of the Civil Evidence (Family Mediation) (Scotland) Act 1995 (inadmissibility in civil proceedings of information as to what occurred during family mediation)–

> *(a) the words from "a" to "wife" shall form paragraph (a) of that subsection; and*
> *(b) after "wife" there shall be added "; or*
> > *(c) two persons who are not civil partners of each other but are living together as if they were civil partners.".*

Though the Civil Partnership Act 2004 contains amendments to the Civil Evidence (Family Mediation) (Scotland) Act 1995, bringing family mediation between civil partners within its terms, these amendments did not also bring same-sex cohabitants within the 1995 Act. There was, as we have already seen, substantial confusion throughout the drafting and enacting of the 2004 Act as to whether rules relating to cohabiting (ie non-registering) same-sex partners should be included and this confusion is illustrated by the omission of same-sex cohabitants from the amended 1995 Act. But the gap is filled here. Family mediation has long been offered in practice to cohabitants, whether opposite-sex or same-sex, and the two categories of couple are now entitled to the same degree of evidentiary privilege that is the purpose of the 1995 Act.

Schedule 2, para 8: Minor and consequential amendments

In subsection (4) of section 12 of the Children (Scotland) Act 1995 (restrictions on decrees for divorce, separation or annulment affecting children)–

> *(a) the existing words from "the parties" to the end shall become paragraph (a) (with the existing paragraphs (a) and (b) becoming subparagraphs (i) and (ii); and*
> *(b) after the new paragraph (a), there shall be added "; or*
> > *(b) the partners in a civil partnership, means a child who has been treated by both partners as a child of the family which their partnership constitutes.".*

This provision is required not to fill a gap left by the Civil Partnership Act 2004 but to remove a distinction deliberately but unnecessarily created between marriage and civil partnership. Section 12 of the Children (Scotland) Act 1995 requires the court to consider whether to make a s 11 order over children when their parents are being divorced. "Children" in this context includes not only children of both spouses but also children of one (or of neither) who have been *treated* by both spouses as children of their family. The 2004 Act amended this provision to provide a similar – but crucially different – rule for civil partners. Of course, civil partners will seldom have children of whom they are both parents (this would only be possible if a same-sex couple adopted a child in England and Wales and then moved to Scotland where the adoption would be automatically recognised, or a foreign adoption order were recognised here). The normal scenario when civil partners are bringing up a child will be that one is parent and the other is not. In that situation the court's obligation to consider making a s 11 order was originally stated in the 2004 Act to apply when both civil partners *accepted*, as opposed to *treated*, the child as a child of their family. There was no conceivable need to make this distinction (which was also made in relation to occupancy rights of civil partners and their children (s 101(7) of the 2004 Act, as originally enacted)) between children being brought up by same-sex couples and children being brought up by opposite-sex couples and the purpose of the present amendment is to achieve what the 2004 Act ought to have done in the first place. (The equivalent amendment to s 101(7) of the 2004 Act, contained in Sch 2, para 3, is discussed above at pp 85–86.) From now on, the court's obligation under s 12 of the Children (Scotland) Act 1995 in dealing with a dissolution of a civil partnership where there are children involved is identical to that when it is dealing with a divorce where there are children involved. And that is, of course, exactly as it should be and should have been.

7 JURISDICTION AND PRIVATE INTERNATIONAL LAW

SECTIONS 37–41

Given the increased mobility of families in the modern world, it is no surprise that foreign law is affecting family life more and more. Jurisdiction, even in family matters, is increasingly being governed within the European Union by Regulations applicable across the member states, as is the mutual recognition of court decrees. However, family connections are in practice as likely to be made in Commonwealth countries, or in the USA, as in Europe and EU Regulations may not apply. In addition, choice of law issues arise even within the European Union. This final substantive part of the Family Law (Scotland) Act 2006 is designed to put onto a statutory basis various choice of law rules concerning aspects of family law, the most important of which are contained in s 38 which deals with choice of law in relation to the validity of marriage. The first section of this part, however, deals with an aspect of jurisdiction.

37 Jurisdiction: actions for declarator of recognition of certain foreign decrees

(1) The Domicile and Matrimonial Proceedings Act 1973 (c. 45) shall be amended in accordance with subsections (2) and (3).

(2) In section 7 (jurisdiction of Court of Session in certain consistorial causes)–

   (a) in subsection (1)

      (i) for "(2) to (8)" there shall be substituted "(2A) to (10)"; and

      (ii) at the end there shall be inserted–

      "(aa) an action for declarator of recognition, or non-recognition, of a relevant foreign decree.";

   (b) in subsection (3A), after "marriage", where it first occurs, there shall be inserted "or for declarator of recognition, or non-recognition, of a relevant foreign decree"; and

   (c) after subsection (8) there shall be added–

      "(9) In this section, "relevant foreign decree" means a decree of divorce, nullity or separation granted outwith a member state of the European Union.

> *(10) References in subsection (3A) to a marriage shall, in the case of an action for declarator of recognition, or non-recognition, of a relevant foreign decree, be construed as references to the marriage to which the relevant foreign decree relates.".*
>
> (3) In section 8 (jurisdiction of sheriff court in certain consistorial causes)–
>
>   (a) in subsection (1)–
>
>   (i) for "(4)" there shall be substituted "(6)";
>
>   (ii) the words from "an" to the end shall become paragraph (a) of that subsection; and
>
>   (iii) at the end there shall be added "and
>
>   (b) an action for declarator of recognition, or non-recognition, of a relevant foreign decree.";
>
>   (b) in subsection (2), after "divorce" there shall be inserted "or for declarator of recognition, or non-recognition, of a relevant foreign decree"; and
>
>   (c) after subsection (4) there shall be added–
>
>   "(5) In this section, "relevant foreign decree" has the meaning given by section 7(9).
>
>   (6) References in subsection (2) to a marriage shall, in the case of an action for declarator of recognition, or non-recognition, of a relevant foreign decree, be construed as references to the marriage to which the relevant foreign decree relates.".

Jurisdiction within the European Union is governed by EC Regulation 2201/2003 (known colloquially as "Brussells II *bis*"), covering both consistorial actions and actions relating to parental responsibility: additionally, this provides for the automatic enforcement of orders in these matters throughout the European Union (with the exception of Denmark). Equivalent rules in relation to civil partnership are contained in the Civil Partnership (Jurisdiction and Recognition of Judgments) (Scotland) Regulations 2005, SSI 2005/629. If no court has jurisdiction under either set of regulations, the Domicile and Matrimonial Proceedings Act 1973 continues to apply, together with the equivalent rules for civil partners in s 225 of the Civil Partnership Act 2004.

The amendments to the 1973 Act contained in the present pro-vision add to the scope of that Act by including within it actions for declarator of recognition or non-recognition of decrees of divorce, nullity or separation from courts outwith the European Union and are designed to ensure that such actions can be raised in either the Court of Session or the sheriff court under the existing rules. Recognition or non-recognition of dissolution or annulment of civil partnership (but curiously not separation) is governed by SSI 2005/629.

38 Validity of marriages

(1) Subject to the Foreign Marriage Act 1892 (c. 23), the question whether a marriage is formally valid shall be determined by the law of the place where the marriage was celebrated.

(2) The question whether a person who enters into a marriage–

(a) had capacity; or

(b) consented,

to enter into it shall, subject to subsections (3) and (3A) and to section 50 of the Family Law Act 1986 (c. 55) (non-recognition of divorce or annulment in another jurisdiction no bar to remarriage), be determined by the law of the place where, immediately before the marriage, that person was domiciled.

(3) If a marriage entered into in Scotland is void under a rule of Scots internal law, then, notwithstanding subsection (2), that rule shall prevail over any law under which the marriage would be valid.

(4) The capacity of the person to enter into the marriage shall not be determined under the law of the place where, immediately before the marriage, the person was domiciled in so far as it would be contrary to public policy in Scotland for such capacity to be so determined.

(5) If the law of the place in which a person is domiciled requires a person under a certain age to obtain parental consent before entering into a marriage, that requirement shall not be taken to affect the capacity of a person to enter into a marriage in Scotland unless failure to obtain such consent would render invalid any marriage that the person purported to enter into in any form anywhere in the world.

The choice of law rules for marriage have never been entirely clear though such Scottish judicial authority as existed suggested, and a clear preponderance of academic opinion concurred in the suggestion, that a distinction required to be made between formal validity (which was governed by the law of the *lex loci celebrationis* or the place of the celebration) and essential validity (which was governed by the law of the domicile of each party). This approach is now put onto a statutory basis here. Formal validity includes matters such as who can conduct the ceremony, the civil notices required, age and number of witnesses and subs (1) provides that the law of the place where the marriage is celebrated governs these matters (subject to the rules in the 1892 Act which allows the UK authorities to solemnise a marriage abroad using UK formalities if at least one of the parties is a UK national – similar rules for civil partnership are contained in the regulations made under ss 239–242 of the 2004 Act, as for example the Civil Partnership (Armed Forces) Order 2005 SI 2005/3188). Essential validity concerns matters of capacity to marry and validity of consent and both these matters are, under subs (2), governed by the domicile of the person whose capacity or consent is in question. Treating validity of consent in the same way as capacity resolves a doubt at common law as to whether the former was a matter for the law of the domicile or for the *lex loci celebrationis*. The most recent decision was very firmly to the effect that validity of consent was a matter for the law of the domicile (*Singh* v *Singh* 2005 SLT 749) and the new statutory rule reflects this approach.

This double rule (formalities governed by the place of celebration; capacity and consent governed by the domicile of each party) applies, in the wording of subss (1) and (2), to all marriages but its effect is felt only in relation to marriages that take place abroad, for when a marriage takes place in Scotland the *lex loci* (the law of Scotland, as contained in the Marriage (Scotland) Act 1977) claims to govern various aspects of capacity and consent as well as formality and, indeed, that claim is given statutory effect by subs (3), though only where the Scottish rule is less generous than the foreign rule. So for example a person from a country where the age of marriage is 15 cannot rely on subs (2) of the present section to trump, as it were, the rule in s 1(2) of the Marriage (Scotland) Act 1977 that a marriage in Scotland before both parties are 16 is void; a person who is capable by their domiciliary law but incapable in our eyes of understanding the nature of marriage cannot rely on subs (2) to trump the rule in s 20A(3)(a) of the 1977 Act (as inserted by s 2 of the present Act) that a marriage in Scotland is void if either party is so incapable. If, however, the Scottish rule is more generous in terms of capacity than the law of the domicile, it will be the law of the domicile that governs: if, for example, a person is domiciled in a country where the age of marriage is 18 then subs (2) prevents that person from validly marrying in Scotland before attaining that age, because they are not capable by the law of their domicile. This reflects, and is consistent with, the rule in s 5(4)(f) of the 1977 Act that there is an impediment to marriage in Scotland if one of the parties is subject to a domiciliary incapacity. And it is to be remembered that a marriage that is invalid by the law of the place (outwith Scotland) where it was celebrated may be saved by the doctrine of marriage by cohabitation with habit and repute if the conditions in s 3(3) and (4) of the present Act are satisfied.

Subsection (4) contains a public policy exception to recognition of foreign capacity, though it is worded rather oddly. Normally, a statutory public policy exception to the application of a foreign rule focuses on the rule itself which is said to be obnoxious to our principles. An example is s 218 of the Civil Partnership Act 2004 under which an overseas civil partnership is not to be recognised as valid if it would be manifestly contrary to public policy to recognise the capacity, under the law of the country where the partnership was registered, of one or other of the partners. The present provision, however, focuses not on the foreign rule of law but on the choice of the foreign legal system itself: capacity is not to be determined by the law of country X if it would be contrary to public policy to allow country X to determine capacity. One would have expected the rule to be that a particular capacity or incapacity would not be recognised if the result of doing so would be unacceptable (for example capacity were too generous, as in recognising the capacity of young children to marry, or incapacity were too severe, as in recognising an incapacity to marry imposed for punitive, or racial, reasons). However, the wording of the present provision (unlike that relating to civil partnership) allows the Scottish court to disapply a foreign *in*capacity as well as a foreign capacity (because incapacity is as much part of "the law of the place" as is capacity).

Once a foreign rule has been disapplied, or the legal system deemed inapplicable, for public policy reasons this still leaves the question of whether the person is capable of marrying, or (more accurately) which legal system is left to determine that question. If, for example, a citizen of Gondwanaland married at an age below that set in Scots domestic law, the law of that country permitting this, the Scottish court might well wish to refuse to recognise the marriage on public policy grounds. But applying subs (4) simply means that we would not recognise Gondwanaland's right to determine the person's capacity to marry – it does *not* mean that we would not recognise the person's capacity. So the question arises: if Gondwanaland does not determine the person's capacity, which legal system does? There are only two alternatives: either it is the *lex loci celebrationis* or the law of the forum that determines capacity if the law of the domicile is not to be allowed to do so. The former approach receives some support from the fact that it is that law that determines capacity for civil partnership (Civil Partnership Act 2004, s 215(1)) and indeed it is likely that this law has more connection with the marriage than the law of the forum which is usually entirely fortuitous (normally being determined by contemporary circumstances rather than those that existed at the date of the marriage). The *lex loci* often claims to govern most aspects of capacity in any case (as Scots law does in relation to age, forbidden degrees and (since s 2 above came into force) capacity to understand and to consent to marriage). It follows, it is submitted, that whenever the law of the domicile is disapplied by application of subs (4), the question of whether a person is capable of marrying is to be determined instead by the law of the place where the marriage is celebrated. The Act, curiously, provides no public policy exception if the result of that law too is contrary to public policy (for example if the *lex loci* is the domicile as well, which is a likely scenario) but the common law must provide a safety net here and, at least when a UK jurisdiction is the forum, the *lex fori* as a default position is the only legal system left that can govern the question of capacity.

Subsection (5) gives effect to the common law rule in *Bliersbach* v *MacEwen* 1959 SC 43 that where a foreign parental consent requirement is regarded, by the system that imposes it, as a formality rather than one that removes capacity it will be ignored for marriages in Scotland. The statutory formulation of the rule may well be rather broader than the common law principle, for it creates a presumption that a parental consent requirement will be ignored in Scotland, unless it can be shown that it is an unavoidable requirement which the domiciliary law imposes no matter where the marriage takes place. There is no equivalent rule for civil partnership notwithstanding that most legal systems (including England and Wales, and Northern Ireland: see the Civil Partnership Act 2004, ss 4 and 145) that have introduced civil partnership have replicated parental consent provisions. Matters of both capacity and formality are governed, according to the UK private international law rules for recognition of foreign civil partnership, by the *lex loci registrationis* (2004 Act, s 215) and for civil partnerships registered in Scotland there is no parental consent requirement, even when one or both partners is domiciled in a country where such consent would be an absolute requirement. See further, Norrie, "Recognition of Foreign Relationships under the Civil Partnership Act 2004" (2006) Journal of Private International Law 137.

39 Matrimonial property

> (1) Any question in relation to the rights of spouses to each other's immoveable property arising by virtue of the marriage shall be determined by the law of the place in which the property is situated.
>
> (2) Subject to subsections (4) and (5), if spouses are domiciled in the same country, any question in relation to the rights of the spouses to each other's moveable property arising by virtue of the marriage shall be determined by the law of that country.
>
> (3) Subject to subsections (4) and (5), if spouses are domiciled in different countries then, for the purposes of any question in relation to the rights of the spouses to each other's moveable property arising by virtue of the marriage, the spouses shall be taken to have the same rights to such property as they had immediately before the marriage.
>
> (4) Any question in relation to–
>> (a) the use or occupation of a matrimonial home which is moveable; or

    (b) *the use of the contents of a matrimonial home (whether the home is moveable or immoveable),*

    shall be determined by the law of the country in which the home is situated.

(5) *A change of domicile by a spouse (or both spouses) shall not affect a right in moveable property which, immediately before the change, has vested in either spouse.*

(6) *This section shall not apply–*

    (a) *in relation to the law on aliment, financial provision on divorce, transfer of property on divorce or succession;*

    (b) *to the extent that spouses agree otherwise.*

(7) *In this section, "matrimonial home" has the same meaning as in section 22 of the 1981 Act.*

This section (*pace* the headnote) is not concerned with "matrimonial property" in the technical sense as defined by s 10(4) of the Family Law (Scotland) Act 1985 and as such the use of the phrase is unfortunate. The section is concerned with property, whenever acquired, owned by the parties to a marriage and it is designed not to give any rule of ownership in such property but solely to identify which legal system governs ownership and disposal if questions arise in a particular way.

Some legal systems recognise far more proprietorial effects of marriage than Scots law in the modern age does where, to a large extent, property effects of marriage are limited to the end of marriage, by death or divorce – situations explicitly excluded from the rules in this section. Yet disputes might come before the Scottish courts involving parties one or both of whom are domiciled abroad, or over property that is situated abroad: these disputes may be between the marriage parties themselves or between a spouse and a third party (such as a creditor). The purpose of the present section is to clarify matters rather than to change the common law when any dispute arises concerning the rights each spouse has in property that either or both own. The simplest rule concerns immoveable property: subs (1) requires disputes relating to immoveable property of either spouse to be determined by the law of the place where the property is situated. So if a creditor of a husband, say, is seeking rights over a holiday home that the husband and his wife jointly own in Spain, or Thailand, the question of the wife's protection from the husband's creditors is determined, insofar as the holiday home is concerned, by the law of Spain or, as the case may be, Thailand. This reflects the common law rule: *Welch v Tennent* (1891) 18 R (HL) 72.

The matter is a little more complex in relation to moveable property. If the parties share a common domicile, then the law of that domicile governs any question relating to the right of each in the moveable property of either or both. If, however, they do not share a domicile then their rights in the moveable property are those rights they had immediately before the marriage – in other words, marriage does not affect their rights in each other's movable property. This clarifies an issue of some doubt in the common law where the only authority was to the effect that it was the husband's domicile that governed such questions, but such authority had been rendered suspect after 1973 when married women acquired the capacity to hold an independent domicile (see E M Clive, *Husband and Wife* (4th edn) at paras 14.124–14.134). Though the reference in the new statutory rule is to the rights "to such property" immediately before marriage, this should be read to include property obtained since the date of the marriage: "such property" means property of that nature rather than that property that was owed by either spouse immediately before they married. For otherwise there would be no rule (or a common law rule based on outmoded concepts of a husband's predominance) for subsequently acquired property.

All these rules are subject to the exception that rights of occupancy and use of the matrimonial home (as defined in s 22 of the Matrimonial Homes (Family Protection) (Scotland) Act 1981) and its contents (including when the home is moveable and whether the contents are moveable or immoveable) are determined by the law of the place where the matrimonial home is situated.

This section is limited to marriage and is not extended to civil partnership. The common law, knowing nothing of civil partnership, did not of course develop any private international law rules relating to partnership property and any rights of civil partners in each other's property need to be traced to the Civil Partnership Act 2004 itself. That Act, however, contains no rules analogous to those in the present section and the courts may not be able to develop similar principles for civil partners given that in most countries of the world the relationship would not be recognised at all. Nevertheless, there seems little doubt that, in relation to immoveable property, it will be for the *lex situs* to determine whether the relationship between the civil partners will have any effect on the question of property rights. Similarly, when the partners share a domicile it will be for the *lex domicilii* to allow the relationship to affect, or not, property rights. The difficult case will be where the partners are domiciled in different countries one of which recognises property effects of the relationship and one of which does not. The court could follow the marriage rule in subs (3), or it could apply its own law as the *lex fori*, or it could adopt the law of the country where the moveable property is situated. The issue is unlikely to arise often (at least until more countries introduce civil partnership) and the easiest rule is one based on the *lex fori*. If UK law recognises the civil partnership and the action is raised in the UK then there is much to be said in favour of the simplicity of letting choice of law follow jurisdiction. If forum shopping (the great counter-argument to any *lex fori* approach) becomes a problem then our Parliament can act to resolve it. The greater risk is that the end result for civil partners will be different (through the application of different legal systems) from married couples in exactly the same circumstances. The failure to extend the *lex loci* rule to moveable family homes of civil partners may prove particularly troublesome here.

40 Aliment

Subject to the Maintenance Orders (Reciprocal Enforcement) Act 1972 (c. 18), a court in Scotland shall apply Scots internal law in any action for aliment which comes before it.

There was common law authority to the effect that the law of the mother's domicile governed her liability to aliment her child (*Macdonald* v *Macdonald* (1846) 8 D 830; *Rosses* v *Sinhjee* (1891) 19 R 31) and doubtless the same principle applied to a father's obligation. The rule was inconvenient and potentially unfair if the child lived in a different jurisdiction from the parent/payer. Even more inconvenient was the fact that in alimentary actions between spouses the applicable rule seemed to be different and the law of the forum applied rather than the law of the domicile of the payer (*Pearce* v *Pearce* (1898) 5 SLT 338; *Allum* v *Allum* 1965 SLT (Sh Ct) 26). The Scottish Law Commission suggested in its 1992 Report on *Family Law* (at para 18.5) that the substantive law should follow jurisdiction, and this section gives effect to that recommendation. It applies to any action for aliment brought under the Family Law (Scotland) Act 1985, whether by a child, spouse or civil partner, though actions to enforce overseas decrees remain governed by the Maintenance Orders (Reciprocal Enforcement) Act 1972.

41 Effect of parents' marriage in determining status to depend on law of domicile

Any question arising as to the effect on a person's status of–

(a) *the person's parents being, or having been, married to each other; or*

(b) *the person's parents not being, or not having been, married to each other,*

shall be determined by the law of the country in which the person is domiciled at the time at which the question arises.

Section 21 of the present Act abolishes the status of illegitimacy insofar as a person's status is governed by Scots law. If domiciled elsewhere, it is the law of that domicile that determines whether the person's status is affected by whether or not his or her parents are or were married to each other. By wording this provision in terms of status rather than legitimacy, the Act avoids the old common law conundrum that legitimacy was determined by domicile while domicile was determined by legitimacy (or otherwise). A child's domicile is now determined by the Scottish courts without regard to the marriage status of his or her parents (s 22 above); if that domicile, once determined, then allows the child's status to be affected by the question of parental marriage, Scots law will accept that effect on status, though of course this will not have any effects on any matter governed by the internal law of Scotland. But if, say, the person's succession rights are affected by his or her parents' marital status in the law of his or her domicile, Scots law will apply the domiciliary law, including recognising the effects on status that that foreign law has.

INDEX

same-sex cohabitants (*cont*)
  Civil Evidence (Family Mediation)
    (Scotland) Act 1995, extension of,
    92
  Damages (Scotland) Act 1976,
    extension of, 88–90
  generally, 83–93
  Matrimonial Homes (Family
    Protection) (Scotland) Act 1981,
    extension of, 86–88
  occupancy rights and, 86–88
Scottish Law Commission Reports,
  xv
separation
  balancing lump sum, claim for,
    68–69
  future child-care costs, 69–72
  generally, 65–67, 72
  periods of, for divorce, reduction in,
    27–28
"sham marriages", 6
sheriff clerks, execution of deeds by, 40

special destinations, revocation on
  divorce or annulment
  civil partners, 41
  spouses, 40–41, 42
spouses, occupancy rights of
    court action, effect of, 21
    duration, 14
    "matrimonial home",
      amendment of definition,
      22–23
    third parties, dealings with, 15,
    18

unmarried fathers, parental
  responsibilities and parental rights
  of, 50–53

void civil partnerships, 4
void marriages
  consent, lack of, for, 3–4, 5–6
  duress, for, 5
  error, for, 3–4

Printed and bound by CPI Group (UK) Ltd, Croydon, CR0 4YY

23/03/2025

01835763-0001